GOD'S SUPERIOR WOMAN

GOD'S SUPERIOR WOMAN

EDWARD LEE JOHNSON SR.

GOD'S SUPERIOR WOMAN by Edward Lee Johnson Sr.
Published by Creation House
A Strang Company
600 Rinehart Road
Lake Mary, Florida 32746
www.creationhouse.com

This book or parts thereof may not be reproduced in any form, stored in a retrieval system, or transmitted in any form by any means—electronic, mechanical, photocopy, recording, or otherwise—without prior written permission of the publisher, except as provided by United States of America copyright law.

Unless otherwise noted, all Scripture quotations are from the King James Version of the Bible.

Scripture quotations marked NLT are from the Holy Bible, New Living Translation, copyright © 1996. Used by permission of Tyndale House Publishers, Inc., Wheaton, IL 60189. All rights reserved.

Scripture quotations marked TLB are from The Living Bible. Copyright © 1971. Used by permission of Tyndale House Publishers, Inc., Wheaton, IL 60189. All rights reserved.

Cover design by Terry Clifton

Copyright © 2007 by Edward Lee Johnson Sr.
All rights reserved

Library of Congress Control Number: 2006939056
International Standard Book Number-13: 978-1-59979-164-7

First Edition

07 08 09 10 11 — 987654321
Printed in the United States of America

The entire Destiny 2000 and Beyond Family Series is dedicated to my wife and six children, my dad, my siblings, and a host of relatives. These books also celebrate the memory of my mother, who is resting with God. "We are family."

Contents

Introduction 1
1 The Daughters of Zion 7
2 We Are Family 31
3 Mother Knows Best 45
4 Suffering From Within 57
5 It's the Lady in You 73
6 My Girlfriends 85
7 Building Her Community 97
8 We Are Leaders Too 107
9 The Professional Woman 117
10 Guarding Your Health 135
11 Women in the Word 147
12 Women in Ministry 165

INTRODUCTION

WHAT IS INTERESTING ABOUT this book is that until I wrote the previous seven books in the Destiny 2000 and Beyond Family Series, I did not envision this book as a further addition to that series. When I began writing the series only eleven months ago, I was still grieving over my mother, who had just gone home to be with God. That this series exists is a miracle; what started out as an early morning wakeup call from God has turned out to be a life's work written in eight books. My current plan calls for a ninth and final volume, but if God inspires me to continue, of course, I will obey.

This book is designed for women, and as the fifty-one-year-old son of a pastor's wife, I think I have some insight into the female mind. However, to supplement my experience, I have taken the liberty of polling other women—including my wife—to find the appropriate topics to talk about. Needless to say, women have played an indispensable role in building every area of our society. The Destiny 2000 and Beyond Family Series would not be complete without a book for women. I am going to take the liberty to share in this installment every positive thing that I know about females. I want to personally thank all of the ladies that have helped to shape my life and I hope that this book will be a testament to their love, faith, and loyalty to the things of God. The apostle Paul saw fit to reference the mother and grandmother of Timothy in his writings because they made such a great impression upon his life.

I am eternally grateful to my mother for everything she did to help me reach this place in my life. As much as I love my father, it was my mother to whom I turned as a young man for consolation when I was hurting. She knew just what to say to get me back on track. My mother was a traditional housewife; she never worked a job outside the home—at least not for any length of time. She and my father taught my siblings and I how to love God and one another. I remember how she would reprimand us for our childhood spats: "Cats and dogs fight but not sisters and brothers." And she saw to it that we were well-fed every morning before school. Even after all of us were grown and out of the house, Mom still cooked a hot meal every day. She continued to cook until she got sick and was unable to work in the kitchen. Her kindness extended beyond our immediate family; she was very active in our community and would help anyone who needed a hand. She never knew a stranger, and she knew how to make one feel welcome in her presence. If she thought someone wanted something of hers, she would freely give it.

I also remember my mother working in the church alongside my dad. Though she was not the type to do much from the sacred podium, she was very active in the background. Mom was an active prayer warrior and saw to it that we learned the value of prayer early in our lives. I remember my mother and a few of my aunts taking many of us as young children to the church for noonday prayer. We would all gather around the altar and pray until the glory of the Lord filled the house. As children, we did not fully understand what this meant, but as we grew older, it proved to be a good foundation for us.

Mom traveled with my father almost everywhere he went, carrying the gospel to many churches and communities. She and my dad would sing duets while he played the guitar. In those days, many people visited our home; some stayed for a night and others for weeks. My mother welcomed them into our house as if they were family. She would get up early in the morning and see to it that they had breakfast, cooking it herself. This book will probably model her legacy in many ways; she was just that special to her family, the church, and the community.

Much of the sense of family, and the attendant family values, that I grew up with are things of the past in many communities. As I begin to comprehend and focus in on what God was doing when He birthed the Destiny 2000 and Beyond Family Series in my spirit, I see that He wanted me to capture those family values for many who were not privileged to enjoy this kind of lifestyle. Both in the church and in the world at large, people are suffering because they don't have a clue as to what it takes to build a structured life. And many of the families who have managed to do well have not learned to share their success with their communities. Selfishness has permeated most of our ministries and the focus has shifted from the community to personal aggrandizement. What we need more than anything else is for the basic values of family and community to resurface in the world.

We need more women with hearts that are big enough to make the sacrifices needed to help others. It really does take a village to raise a child and we have all but abandoned the village for the glamour. In order to build a strong community, we must have women who are not stuck on themselves. Our world needs more women who do not mind sacrificing some of what they have in order to share it with those who are less fortunate. This type of communal spirit allows a community to survive against all odds.

Women of God in the past have given us a foundation that must not be erased. It is up to each one of you to begin recapturing those values that God has given us in His Word to model for our day. Christian men could better live out their roles as sons, prophets, priests, and kings if they had their "queens" alongside them. You can make this happen simply by becoming, as the title of this book says, *God's Superior Woman: Conquering Her World Through Love.* The prophet Jeremiah spoke to this very issue; if ever we needed these principles in place, the time is now. Here is what he had to say to the nation of Israel over twenty-five hundred years ago:

> Thus saith the LORD of hosts, Consider ye, and call for the mourning women, that they may come; and send for cunning women, that they may come: And let them make haste, and take up a wailing for us, that our eyes may run down with tears, and our eyelids gush out with waters. For a voice of wailing is heard out of Zion,

> How are we spoiled! we are greatly confounded, because we have forsaken the land, because our dwellings have cast us out. Yet hear the word of the Lord, O ye women, and let your ear receive the word of his mouth, and teach your daughters wailing, and every one her neighbour lamentation. For death is come up into our windows, and is entered into our palaces, to cut off the children from without, and the young men from the streets. Speak, Thus saith the Lord, Even the carcases of men shall fall as dung upon the open field, and as the handful after the harvestman, and none shall gather them. Thus saith the Lord, Let not the wise man glory in his wisdom, neither let the mighty man glory in his might, let not the rich man glory in his riches: But let him that glorieth glory in this, that he understandeth and knoweth me, that I am the Lord which exercise lovingkindness, judgment, and righteousness, in the earth: for in these things I delight, saith the Lord.
>
> —Jeremiah 9:17–24

I once heard a mother say, "Since men are blaming women for getting the world in trouble through Eve, we need to be the ones who get it out of trouble through love." God's superior women are above average, better quality, and more advanced than others in the things of God and His kingdom. If you are not a superior woman at this point in your life, reading this book and adopting the principles in it will guarantee your place in history among the superior women of the world. Being superior does not mean being most noticeable in the eyes of men. What it does mean is that your life will measure up to the quality of women who know their places in God and will not deviate from this course of righteousness in order to impress people. The superior woman does the right thing, not the popular thing. She does what is honest, not what is convenient. She loves not only those who love her, but also her enemies. She seeks out the weak, downtrodden, sick, abused, and those who are hurting in order to ameliorate their pain through the love of Christ.

When the Lord shall have washed away the filth of the daughters of Zion, and shall have purged the blood of Jerusalem from the midst thereof by the spirit of judgment, and by the spirit of burning.

—Isaiah 4:4

Chapter 1

THE DAUGHTERS OF ZION

The daughters of Zion are those women of God who have a passion for the kingdom to come and are willing to serve, give, pray, and carry the gospel to the corners of the earth, starting with their families.

THE TERM *ZION* MEANS "fortification of stronghold." It was a site in Jerusalem where David captured one of the enemies of Israel, the Jebusites. The entire city of Jerusalem eventually became known as Zion. This is where God established his covenant with David to make him king forever. The descendants of David as well as the whole house of Judah became the people of Zion. David's roots lay in the tribe of Judah, which was formed from the two southern tribes that stood for over a century after the fall of the ten northern tribes known as Israel. Zion, also known as the city of David, would ultimately become the most controversial piece of real estate on the face of the planet. It became the place where the covenant and laws of God, made to His covenant people, would be held dear and precious for eternity.

One would think that after the coming of the Messiah, who sanctioned it as the model city for the world, Jerusalem would be flourishing with peace and prosperity. Unfortunately, on any given day, one can still read and watch the news and see that we have not yet learned the true purpose of the city.

When the daughters of Zion are restored to their rightful places spiritually, they will be the first of an expedition that will usher the glory of

God back to the holy city. I cannot write enough about how important it is for women to find their places in the kingdom in order to help men find their places. Women by far have superseded men when it comes to passion, love, and hunger for holiness. Here is how the prophet Jeremiah worded it when he prophesied over twenty-five hundred years ago:

> Set thee up waymarks, make thee high heaps: set thine heart toward the highway, even the way which thou wentest: turn again, O virgin of Israel, turn again to these thy cities. How long wilt thou go about, O thou backsliding daughter? for the LORD hath created a new thing in the earth, A woman shall *compass* a man. Thus saith the LORD of hosts, the God of Israel; As yet they shall use this speech in the land of Judah and in the cities thereof, when I shall bring again their captivity; The LORD bless thee, O habitation of justice, and mountain of holiness. And there shall dwell in Judah itself, and in all the cities thereof together, husbandmen, and they that go forth with flocks. For I have satiated the weary soul, and I have replenished every sorrowful soul. Upon this I awaked, and beheld; and my sleep was sweet unto me. Behold, the days come, saith the LORD, that I will sow the house of Israel and the house of Judah with the seed of man, and with the seed of beast.
> —JEREMIAH 31:21–27, EMPHASIS ADDED

It is clear to me that God has a plan for the women who long for Zion, the stronghold of God, to be restored to its rightful place. As I have traveled through the church and many portions of the world, I have found that women make up 60 to 80 percent of most congregations. It is the women who are in the trenches holding the auxiliaries in our churches together. They work harder, pray longer, and give more overall. Any man would be downright foolish to try and hold women back from working in the kingdom of God. You cannot, should not, must not become discouraged by insecure men who don't know how to handle the gift that God has given them in women. I know that there are a few women who want to dominate and upstage men, but this is by far the minority.

I've been in the pastorate for more than half of my life and I am 100 percent sure of what I am saying; I've experienced it firsthand. Let me personally thank you and tell you how much I love and appreciate the work that you do in the kingdom of God. As long as I have breath in my body and I'm able to work in the ministry, I want to have the corporation of women by my side. I sometimes listen to preachers on radio and television degrading women and talking about what God did not call them to do. I simply respond this way: when the men are willing to get up and take their places, the women would not have to do all of the things that they are doing. In the meantime those fellows need to shut up and let God use the person who is willing to do the job. The apostle Paul declares that there is no gender when it comes to the kingdom.

> For ye are all the children of God by faith in Christ Jesus. For as many of you as have been baptized into Christ have put on Christ. There is neither Jew nor Greek, there is neither bond nor free, there is neither male nor female: for ye are all one in Christ Jesus.
> —Galatians 3:26–28

Women, you have a mandate from God to do what you do. I have tried to make this clear to you in the preceding paragraphs, so do not allow yourselves or anyone else to keep you from the blessing that God has for you through your obedience to Him. You are going to be tested and tried in the fire like everyone else, but you have what it takes to be a winner because it is already in your spiritual DNA. If you are going through some testing and processing experiences at the moment, they are all part of the plan of God. The devil has a price of frustration and failure assigned to you, but you must remember these words from the apostle Paul:

> Ye are of God, little children, and have overcome them: because greater is he that is in you, than he that is in the world.
> —1 John 4:4

Aware of Our Past

From the inception of humanity, women have always played a major role in every culture. The very fact that it takes a female to produce offspring tells us that the female gender is an indispensable part of humanity, although history has proven to be very unkind to women in many areas. Even in our present era women are still striving for total equality in society. In many cases a woman can produce the exact same outcome in the workplace and still get less compensation simply because of her gender. This kind of disproportionate contribution to communal wealth is nothing new, and we can see in the Bible the foundation for this mind-set. I'm not suggesting that God is in any way responsible for this chauvinistic and arrogant attitude that many men possess, but I can see how Scripture can be misconstrued. When God issued His judgment upon Eve for her disobedience in the Garden of Eden, one of her punishments was to have her desires made subject to her husband. Here is exactly what the Bible says:

> Unto the woman he said, I will greatly multiply thy sorrow and thy conception; in sorrow thou shalt bring forth children; and thy desire shall be to thy husband, and he shall rule over thee.
> —Genesis 3:16

In my opinion, this very verse, misunderstood and taken out of context, is the origin of all the disparities women have suffered at the hands of men. Unless we go back and rightly interpret what God meant when He gave this command, we will continue this struggle for as long as humanity exists.

The same principle holds true when it comes to the blatant racism that exists against people of color, primarily African-Americans. It has been said that black people are ordained by God to be subservient to whites because the curse of God is upon them, and this is why they have dark skin and their hair is kinky. Here is what the Bible says:

> And Noah awoke from his wine, and knew what his younger son had done unto him. And he said, Cursed be Canaan; a servant of servants shall he be unto his brethren.
>
> —Genesis 9:24–25

Notice that God had nothing to do with this judgment that was passed down by Noah. This was Noah's response to his own weakness being played out in his son Ham. However, God did curse Cain in Genesis 4:11:

> And now art thou cursed from the earth, which hath opened her mouth to receive thy brother's blood from thy hand.

So then, you can clearly see that men's wicked hearts alone have to accept the responsibility for the breakdown in human relations that we are experiencing today.

When God told Eve that she would be ruled by her husband, He never intended for her spouse to be a dictator or a tyrant, but a loving leader functioning with the same kind of love that He has. The problem we are having is that the hearts of many men are weak, evil, and insecure—so they attempt to carry out their roles through force, aggression, and intimidation. The only reason anyone would want to intimidate another human being is because they themselves are weak. Statistics have proven that most women mature faster than men and are usually more compassionate and caring. They operate in a way that is totally different from men when it comes to the way they interpret things. This serious disconnect must be rectified if they are going to get on level ground with men.

I would not be completely honest if I did not tell you that many women can be intimidating to men and really give them a hard way to go in some cases. If a man is already weak and insecure, for a woman to push his buttons would be suicide. Why any woman would press the issue to her own detriment is quite puzzling to me, but I've seen it happen time and time again. In most cases the woman ends up the victim, but often the men lose out, too. If we are going to get this thing together, we're going to have to revisit Scripture and find out just how God intended for the spousal roles to be carried out.

Everything I know about God based on Scripture is that He is loving, caring, and compassionate—and judgmental only as a last resort. If the man is going to properly carry out his role as a husband and rule his wife as the Bible says, he must first find out what the word *rule* means and how to apply it to his personal situation. The word *rule* simply means to set the standard and to take charge. God has clearly passed down His orders to man, and if man is going to carry out the rules, he must first of all be a just man. He cannot be just until he has been justified by God. When Adam fell from grace, the continuity that connected him and God was severed. Consequently, God stopped speaking and Adam was left to fend for himself. He was banished from the presence of God and as a result became easy prey for the archenemy of God, Satan. Now that God is not giving any directives as to how he should live, man has become nothing more than the wild beasts of the fields. Unless his heart is restored to God through faith, grace, and regeneration, he will continue to connive, cheat, defraud, lie, kill, and commit all the other evil acts that we see every day in our society.

Now let's take a look at what God ordered in the beginning according to Ephesians 5:21–25:

> Submitting yourselves one to another in the fear of God. Wives, submit yourselves unto your own husbands, as unto the Lord. For the husband is the head of the wife, even as Christ is the head of the church: and He is the Saviour of the body. Therefore as the church is subject unto Christ, so let the wives be to their own husbands in every thing. Husbands, love your wives, even as Christ also loved the church, and gave himself for it.

You can find this principle repeated again in Colossians 1. Simply put, before the husband can effectively exercise any kind of authority over a woman, he must have the authority of Christ exercised over his life. As long as unregenerated man is trying to exercise control over a woman or anyone else for that matter, we will live in a frustrated world.

The Daughters of Zion

For the men who have done everything in their power to carry out their roles as godly and loving husbands, yet are still being defied and challenged by a disobedient wife, hold your place and you will be avenged by God in one way or another. As we were having Bible study one evening, this question was asked: if Adam had not sinned along with Eve, what would have happened to her? Someone responded, "God would have slain her and given Adam another wife." It sounded good to me, so I agreed. Of course, only God can say for sure what He would have done.

I don't suppose that this will be straightened out by what I have written if Scripture was ignored for all these years, but I do hope that this sheds some light on the misconception that men have superiority when it comes to women. A man can no more make a woman submit to him than God would force us to love Him. Submission and obedience to God are acts of our free will and this is why there is so much suffering in the world today. If all men in authority today would choose to submit their wills to God, we could eradicate world hunger and most of the evil that exists in one year.

In Numbers 27, the story is told about the daughters of Zelophehad, who came to Moses to petition for their father's inheritance. After seeking God, Moses was instructed to give the land to his daughters because this was the right thing to do. Even during a period in history when men totally dominated society, God never wavered when it came to justice. The atmosphere was ripe for women to be taken lightly, but God would not let them be treated unfairly. If men simply seek God concerning women functioning alongside them, they will receive His counsel.

> One day the daughters of Zelophehad came to the entrance of the Tabernacle to give a petition to Moses, Eleazar the priest, the tribal leaders, and others who were there. The names of these women were Mahlah, Noah, Hoglah, Milcah, and Tirzah. They were members of the half-tribe of Manasseh (a son of Joseph). Their ancestor was Machir, son of Manasseh. Manasseh's son Gilead was their great-grandfather, his son Hepher was their grandfather, and his

son Zelophehad was their father. "Our father died in the wilderness," they said, "and he was not one of those who perished in Korah's revolt against the Lord—it was a natural death, but he had no sons. Why should the name of our father disappear just because he had no son? We feel that we should be given property along with our father's brothers." So Moses brought their case before the Lord. And the Lord replied to Moses, "The daughters of Zelophehad are correct. Give them land along with their uncles; give them the property that would have been given to their father if he had lived. Moreover, this is a general law among you, that if a man dies and has no sons, then his inheritance shall be passed on to his daughters.

—Numbers 27:1–8, TLB

Throughout the New Testament it is clear that women hold places of equal standing in Christ. The females in the New Testament weren't given the roles of apostles, but they certainly were not made to feel like second-class citizens when it came to their relationship with Him. First of all, God used a woman to birth Christ into the world. He could have very well duplicated what He did in the Book of Genesis. Instead, He put the Word in the womb of a woman for the purpose of carrying, birthing and nurturing Him.

Mary, the mother of Jesus, Mary Magdalene, Mary the sister of Martha, and Martha had an intimate relationship with Jesus just as He had with Peter, James, and John. These same ladies, according to Matthew 28, were the first to hear from the angels about the resurrection of Jesus. When people truly love each other, petty jealousies and rivalries will dissipate. It is the lack of love and understanding that has this world so messed up.

The kingdom of God coming to Earth is what it's going to take to get us refocused on God. It is clear to me all through Scripture that God is neither a bigot nor a sexist. He is God. When you understand the roles of Adam and Eve you will see that they were created equal and not one over the other. They were equal with different roles. I suppose that this is the crux of the problem: people not knowing their roles. If the man would function properly in the place that God has ordained for him and the woman would do the same, we would not have a problem. God is not the author of confusion, but of peace.

Called to Holiness

Everything we know about the holiness movement in the modern era can be traced back to the end of the nineteenth and the turn of the twentieth century in Los Angeles. That was the birthplace of the Azusa Street Revival. A young black man, who sat under the teachings of holiness from a white man, was the catalyst for what could be called the second greatest revival in history, after the Day of Pentecost. Nearly six hundred million Pentecostals and Charismatics trace their beginning to this era. Charles Parham, preaching the gospel of holiness but still bound in the chains of racism, reluctantly allowed William Seymore to attend his teaching sessions. Seymore, being used by God, was the leading character; he, along with some women and eventually a few whites, started a service in an old building in the industrial area of Azusa Street. This was the humble beginning that spawned the revival of the century. You can read more about this great event on the internet.

Let's talk about the term *holiness*. One of the major breakdowns in the church arena today is the true meaning of holiness. In my opinion, we are out of balance when it comes to principles of holiness. It simply means to be set apart exclusively for the use of God. It could be applied to a person, persons, or things. The priests and Levites, who were responsible for carrying out their duties in the tabernacle and the temple, were charged by Moses from God to be totally involved in ministry and not to hold a secular job. They were not allowed to acquire personal property or work in the fields; they were to be dedicated to the work of God in the temple. Additionally, the nation as a whole was called to holiness. They were called to be a model nation, set apart from the nations that surrounded them. Their practices were to exemplify the very God that they followed in faith. Israel was the only nation that practiced monotheism, the worship of only one God. Abraham, the father and founder of the nation, grew up in a land that was pagan and God called him out and directed him to a place that would ultimately become the land of Israel. The terms *holy, holiness, sanctification, consecration,* and *dedication* all have a common meaning. This is the essence and only meaning of the word *holiness*. So then, how did we get from this to all of the external things that we use to describe the term *holiness* in our modern era? I'm glad you asked; let's deal with it.

We dealt with the resurfacing of the holiness movement at the beginning of this so let's get right to the point of emphasis. In an attempt to interpret Scripture based on what we believe they are trying to convey, we usually start from where we are—historically and culturally—and not necessarily where the writers who wrote the sacred text were. With this in mind, and knowing that the interpreters of our day did not have much knowledge of biblical history, they brought to their interpretations what they best understood the text to mean during that time. In an attempt to sever themselves from the world, they interpreted it to mean not doing anything that the people of the world did, not looking the way they looked, and not going to places where they went. Consequently, almost all of the emphasis on holiness became misconstrued.

Now that we all know holiness is not what you look like but what you live like, how do we go back and correct the erroneous teachings and traditions that we have held for fifty or more years about true holiness? It's not simple to do. Traditions have been known to carry so much weight that the courts will even decide cases based on tradition rather than the law itself. Tradition got Jesus in a whole lot of trouble, even to the point of being put to death. Tradition is known as the customary way of doing things. If it was practiced by those before us, we believe it must be right. Unfortunately, tradition is so strong that if you believe it for long enough, you would rather have tradition than truth. For years we have taught things as a matter of conviction that were nothing more than condemnation. If you know your Bible at all, you know that condemnation was the last thing Jesus came to do. He said that the world was condemned already before He arrived, so His job was to liberate.

The Daughters of Zion

The Old Testament law had lived out much of its purpose, so Jesus' place was to get us free from the laws and traditions that had absolutely no purpose when it came to salvation. In essence, He came to get us out of the wagons and into the cars, from the Paul Revere ride to telephones and computers, and from the clothes you wear to the lifestyle you live in those clothes.

As a lad growing up in church, I remember that living a holy life meant no sports, no movies, little or no television. Men wore bow ties, and women could not wear jewelry—not even a chain to hold their glasses—or any type of make up, and to wear pants was the "sin of the century." The only problem with all of these interpretations is that none of them are based in Scripture; they had simply become tradition. Now that I'm older, fifty-one to be exact, I do understand many of the reasons for these teachings. I'm no fool; the idea behind them was that if you weren't able to decipher the difference between external signs and internal attitude on your own, it was better off for you to follow the teachings than to become entrapped by the enemy. Going to some of these places and doing some of these things could have been a way for the enemy to lure you from your base and get you to lose your way in God. The saints of that era were doing all that they thought was good for the time and I would be the last to speak against their intentions. Now that we know better, we can do better and we should get better results. If staying away from games and movies and not wearing pants is going to keep you saved, you would be better off not going and doing these things. However, if you have grown to a level of spiritual maturity, bring balance to your teachings and stop building roadblocks that God never gave us the authority to build. Let's continue to sound the alarm of holiness and let the world know that it is still holiness or hell—but teach them what true holiness is, the life that you live every day.

The issue of women wearing pants has been a major stumbling block among us as Full Gospel and Pentecostal believers, and I want to give you my personal view on the topic. Perhaps the pants in themselves is not sinful, but I can understand what the older saints were trying to defend. Many of our young women and some of the older ones are wearing their pants so tight that it looks as if they were painted on their bodies. The Bible admonishes us to dress in modest apparel, and if your pants are so revealing that it causes men to lust after your body, you may be responsible for leading someone astray. As men, we have been designed to be visual and appreciate the beauty of women. All men have a weakness when it comes to female sexuality and we need you as women to help us as much as possible. If you are well-built, with nice hips and thighs, which are sex symbols in the eyes of most men, that part of your body should not be exposed to anyone except your spouse. Being feminine and sexy should not mean being enticing and seductive. If you use sensuality to attract men, one day you may not be able to compete when nature sets in at an older age. It is your inner and hidden beauty of the heart that God intends for you to put out front. As God's superior woman, let holiness reign and let your light shine so men might see your good works, not your body.

You can wear a dress down to your ankles and still be as mean as a snake. You can wear a collar turned around backwards and still have a two hundred dollar pornography bill when you leave the holiness convention. You can stay away from basketball and football games and then consume hours of sports television in your living room. You can say that every single song made by a secular artist is sinful and then sing along to the same song when a so-called Christian artist sings it. You can say that quartet music is the only true music and know that many of the same singers are cigar smokers and skirt chasers. This sounds very hypocritical to me, and I know that is not what you want.

So then, if we are going back to holiness, let's do it the biblical way. The Bible says it is an abomination for a woman to wear that which pertains to a man, but in the culture at the time no one wore pants. When it says, "A highway shall be there…and it shall be…called The way of holiness" (Isa. 35:8), it was talking about a people who have had their heart changed as a result of the gospel and not a litany of church rules that mean-spirited people use to control people they would otherwise

The Daughters of Zion

have no influence over. I've said a lot, and I know it's hot, but the truth will set you free, so take it like a bitter pill, it will do you good.

Time is too hot, eternity is too long, and the souls of men are far too important for us to be arguing over petty issues that have no spiritual or eternal value. There are millions of souls that are going to hell for every minute we spend shutting the doors to the kingdom, and somebody will have to answer to God for deliberately misleading people. This is the generation that is called to usher in the kingdom of God; how are we going to justify how we have made the Word of God of no effect by our church's dogma and traditions? What I want to see more than anything else is our communities cleaned up from the filth of illicit sex, drugs, violence, corrupt music, lying politicians, homosexuality, and conniving church folks with their own agendas. We need the power of the gospel to be preached in every street across America where the people who really need it the most can benefit.

We need to get rid of some of the tradition and deal with the condition of the heart of men. You women who can't find a place to preach or teach in the pulpit of a church have a wide open door and a ready-made audience in the streets. Jesus is on His way back and He is coming for a bride who has cleansed herself of the filth of this society. We need cunning women who know how to get a prayer through, women who are not filled with a whole lot of gossip and drama. We need women who know how to dress modestly and don't go into the streets or the church looking like they are trying to entice a man.

> Moreover the LORD saith, Because the daughters of Zion are haughty, and walk with stretched forth necks and wanton eyes, walking and mincing as they go, and making a tinkling with their feet: Therefore the LORD will smite with a scab the crown of the head of the daughters of Zion, and the LORD will discover their secret parts. In that day the Lord will take away the bravery of their tinkling ornaments about their feet, and their cauls, and their round tires like the moon, The chains, and the bracelets, and the mufflers, The bonnets, and the ornaments of the legs, and the

headbands, and the tablets, and the earrings, The rings, and nose jewels, The changeable suits of apparel, and the mantles, and the wimples, and the crisping pins, The glasses, and the fine linen, and the hoods, and the vails. And it shall come to pass, that instead of sweet smell there shall be stink; and instead of a girdle a rent; and instead of well set hair baldness; and instead of a stomacher a girding of sackcloth; and burning instead of beauty.

—Isaiah 3:16–24

Praise and Worship

Women have led the way in praise and worship for the past century and their work is far from over. I've shared with you the special place that God has for you so that you can lead the way in this area. The men will eventually catch up, but you cannot wait for them and jeopardize the reward God wants to give you for your role in the game. Keep the praise and worship flowing because it is the very foundation for the revival that is already under way in the spirit realm. There are some assignments that can only be carried out by you, so you must stay the course and worship God through praise at every opportunity that comes your way.

Praise and worship has become a household phrase in charismatic religious circles. When I was growing up in the church it was called devotional service. Popular Christian music has spiraled upward to the point where it rivals secular music. During the average praise and worship setting, the audience is being entertained by the praise team as opposed to ushering in true worship. When the music and the singing override the worshipers, it becomes a show and not worship. A good worship leader will not allow the music to dominate to the point where the praise team is trying to become stars. There is far too much flesh being flaunted in the presence of God.

When we think of praise and worship, the two words are generally used in the same context, but there is a distinct difference between praise and worship. We worship God for who He is, but we praise Him for what He does. Our heritage of praise and worship comes to us from the ancient Hebrew nation of the Old Testament. The act of praise and worship is found throughout Scripture. This is especially true in the psalms. There are one hundred fifty Psalms divided into five sections. The divisions are as follows: 1–42, 43–79, 80–89, 90–106, and 107–150. The Book of Leviticus gives the order of worship and the psalms are focused on praise.

In this segment the child of destiny will learn the true meaning of praise and worship. A true worshiper is one who lives a devoted life on a continual basis. The brief period that we share with others in a worship service is just a public expression of our daily practice. In the words of Jesus, "They that worship him must worship him in spirit and truth" (John 4:24).

What Is Praise?

Praise can be defined as an act of worship or acknowledgment by which the virtues or deeds of another are recognized and extolled. This is expressed when we give praise to one another for a noble deed. When we praise God it is an expression of our gratitude and appreciation to Him for what He does in our lives. As servants of God this is the highest form of our expression to Him. We praise God for what He does, and we worship Him for who He is. We are called to praise God at all times and in all things. Praise is another way of expressing our faith in His ability to effectively handle those areas in our lives that we have no control over.

We are to praise God both for who He is and for what He does. The entire Book of Psalms is a book of praise and worship. Praise is also expressed through adoration and thanksgiving. When the Hebrew nation praised God, it was inclusive of songs and prayers. Many of the psalms were uttered both individually and corporately. The Israelites worshiped with the full intensity of the body, emotions, and will. Psalm 150 describes an all-inclusive act of the entire being.

When I praise, it actually takes me into another zone with God. The Holy Spirit visits my praise session and it seems like I have an angelic host camping out around me. Until you really learn the secret of praise, your life in Christ will only be half of what it could be.

The Hebrew language has many words that its speakers use to express their praise. *Halal*—"shout with a loud noise." *Yadah*—"hold out or extend the hands in worship." *Zamar*—"praise with instruments of music."

When Moses was in the wilderness he told God he would not leave unless His presence went with him. Moses was expressing the heart of every true worshiper. I don't want to live without having the presence of God in my life. I would be too afraid that I would get so far off track that I would lose my soul. If everybody had reverential fear for God, we would not need external forces to keep our communities in control.

Judah was one of the twelve sons of Jacob. The name *Judah* literally means "to praise." Whenever Israel was forced into battle, the tribesmen of Judah would go first because they knew how to praise God before the battle began. Whatever you do, don't ever let anybody or anything keep the praises of God from your lips.

What Is Worship?

Worship is defined as a pledge of commitment, devotion, and reverence to God expressed by bowing in His presence. The word *worship* is a derivative of the old English word *worthship*. It speaks to the very essence of what God is to us. He is Lord and Master and our Redeemer. All that we are and ever will be is accredited to our Creator. To bow in reverence and awe of His presence is a basic requirement of the believer. All of the biblical patriarchs—beginning with Abraham, and continuing through Isaac, Jacob, Joseph, Moses, and Joshua—went down in history as worshipers.

The Book of Leviticus explains what God expected from the people He sanctified in the wilderness. They were to establish the order of the priesthood on Earth. The priest had a direct responsibility to go to God on behalf of the people, as opposed to the prophet who went to the people for God. Knowing how to worship was a matter of life and death.

During the Day of Atonement, celebrated once a year, the priest had to make a sacrifice for the entire nation. If he walked into the presence of God without first sanctifying himself, he would die instantly. Jesus commanded that the true worshipers must worship in spirit and in truth.

Devotional Worship

If you notice, the last three steps are all biblically based. I deliberately outlined it this way so as to focus your attention on first the natural and then the spiritual aspect of your life. All of what we have studied in the previous chapters will have no lasting meaning if you don't get the message of the true author of this book. This letter must be transferred from your head to your heart or it will have no effect on your life. The Holy Spirit of God must translate for you and impress upon you the very essence of what has been written. The importance of your devotional life with God is unparalleled by your relationship with anyone else on this earth. He must be first at all times or your life will be meaningless. Jesus says to us in the Matthew 16:26, "For what is a man profited, if he shall gain the whole world, and lose his own soul? or what shall a man give in exchange for his soul?"

It is imperative that you spend time with your heavenly Father on a daily basis in order to keep these principles dear to your heart. As you get alone with Him feel free to talk to Him just the way you talk to a trusted friend. Tell Him about your innermost feelings and give Him a chance to comfort your soul. When He doesn't answer you right away, don't become discouraged and give up your pursuit. Sometimes He is simply testing your motive to see if you really do trust Him. As sons and daughters of destiny, you will also receive discipline for the purpose of building character. If you surrender your will totally to Him, He will never let you fall. Your tears may flow through the night but He will give you joy before the morning (see Ps. 30:5).

Called to Worship

The call to worship is a formal call to the worshiper during the worship celebration to invoke the presence of God. During this time the congregation and worship leader will responsively recite a worship passage from the Bible. The ultimate purpose of a worship service is to get you to worship. If you sit through a service and do not engage the presence of God, you haven't worshiped; you merely attended church. Everything that exists in the main portion of a service should lead you to the place of worship and into the presence of God. The music, the songs, the Scriptures, and even the message cannot take the place of worship. These are all conduits to usher you into the presence of God. The biblical patriarchs left a legacy of worship unto the Lord that followed the nation throughout history. Abraham built altars in strategic places in Palestine for the purpose of getting into the presence of God. Jacob's Well is where the Samaritan woman told Jesus that the Jews came to worship.

The Prayer Warrior

Prayer is simply an earnest petition from the heart of the believer straight to the heart of God. The apostle Paul admonishes his spiritual son Timothy in 1 Timothy 2:1–2: "I exhort therefore, that, first of all, supplications, prayers, intercessions, and giving of thanks, be made for all men; for kings, and for all that are in authority; that we may lead a quiet and peaceable life in all godliness and honesty." Most Christians pray a one-dimensional prayer. It is usually about a long Santa Claus list of things that we want for ourselves and our family. Your prayer should be inclusive of all the following. *Petition*—"to appeal to someone on your behalf or on the behalf of someone else." *Adoration*—"to love, esteem, adulate, admire, respect or to have high regard." *Confession*—"admits, acknowledges or declares guilt." *Worship*—"to bow down, from the word worthship, which denotes the worthiness of." *Praise*—"to admire, glorify, commend, honor or congratulate." *Thanksgiving*—"to give thanks, express appreciation, or to bless. True worship can only come from the heart."

The Bible declares that man looks on the outward appearance but God looks on the heart. There is much to be said about the heart because it is with the heart that we relate to our heavenly Father. The heart is defined as the inner part of us that feels and expresses emotions. Man is a tripartite being, consisting of body, soul, and spirit. The body is the exterior, which houses the soul. Within the soul you have emotions, heart, and feelings. The soul houses the spirit, which is the real you. Within the spirit lies the will, intellect, and the mind. Hatred, sadness, love, joy, and peace are all expressions of the human heart. Mankind has both a natural and a spiritual heart. The physical heart is what pumps blood throughout the body but the spiritual heart is where we go to connect with our heavenly Father. Both character and personality are expressed from the heart. Character and personality are two distinct manifestations of human emotions. Your character is the real you at all times; it speaks of the very essence of your being. Personality, on the other hand, is what you portray to impress others. It may or may not be the expression of the real you. It is what you allow the person whom you are seeking to influence to see. This deceptive behavior will usually last until the deceiving party is put under pressure. Pressure has a way of bringing out hidden motives and true character.

God's perfect will for mankind is for him to come clean on his own without dishonesty or deceit. David, the reigning king of Israel, committed the worst kind of sin when he committed adultery with Bathsheba and tried to cover it up by having her husband murdered. Uriah could have very well fallen in battle without David's intent to have him killed, but David put him in front of the battle out of the deceitfulness of his heart. From the outside looking in it seems almost impossible for him to commit this atrocious act. However, if you examine your own heart, you may find that you have committed the same sin. Though you may not have committed physical adultery or murder, harboring the thought of adultery or murder will bring the same consequences. We are good at measuring sin on a sliding scale. God on the other hand sees them all the same. The word *heart* is mentioned over seven hundred times in the Bible; in almost every case, it is an admonishment to rid it of its impure thoughts or motives.

When you pray using the above methods, it opens up a whole new world for you to access the presence of God. Praying should be a lifestyle for the believer. As women of faith, you should model the life that you talk about through your daily activities. Your hearts will remain pure if you go to God several times during the day, confessing those things that sometimes get into your spirit. Prayer, worship, praise, confession, and thanksgiving are the ways we wash the window of our soul.

The Superior Woman's Challenge for Chapter 1

1. Zion women must be women of purpose, vision, kingdom, and family; make this your primary goal.

2. If you do not know where you came from, you cannot know where you are heading; become thoroughly aware of the great women in the Bible and begin to model their lifestyles.

3. You have been called to holiness, which is a lifestyle for the women of Zion and not a denomination; strive to live holy every day. Your heavenly Father is watching your every move.

4. You have officially entered the kingdom era, which goes beyond the traditional church; begin to discover the kingdom principles in the Bible and walk in them everywhere you go.

5. The way you dress in public says a lot about what you think of yourself; begin to look closely at your apparel before you leave home so as to not entice men to lust after your body.

6. Your worship should not be limited to a church building, and when you worship, it should include praise, prayer, confession, adoration, petitioning, and thanksgiving.

7. Spend at least twenty minutes alone with God daily in prayer, reading the Bible, and meditating on His Word.

Journal

Use this section to log special events (i.e., spiritual breakthroughs, special messages, meeting of new friends, etc.).

Week 1

_____

_____

_____

_____

_____

_____

Week 2

_____

_____

_____

_____

_____

_____

Week 3

Week 4

Either his uncle, or his uncle's son, may redeem him, or any that is nigh of kin unto him of his family may redeem him; or if he be able, he may redeem himself.

—Leviticus 25:49

Chapter 2

WE ARE FAMILY

> True sisters will disagree, become estranged, debate, and sometimes fight, but love each other just the same. It's called unconditional love.

THE FAMILY IS THE basic structural unit of society. No civil society will survive if it does not continue to promote good family values. We can see from history—starting with the people of the Bible—that God will judge and condemn any nation that destroys this building block of society. Since our culture has been established as Judeo-Christian, we must turn to the legacy in which it was established if we plan to keep God's favor upon the nation. You can turn to the pages of the Bible to find out how, and how not to be, a father, husband, wife, sister, and brother. Although the Bible does not give us a particular family to model, we can learn from the principles throughout its pages how to conduct ourselves towards one another.

The Bible is like a jigsaw puzzle; if you can put the pieces together, you will have a masterpiece. It is a hard thing to have youth and wisdom at the same time. It would serve you well to trust an older person, if not your parents, to give you sound advice for life. As an older person, you can still learn these principles if you humbly seek the wisdom of God. If you follow these twelve principles, you will not go wrong.

I grew up in a rather large family by today's standards. Thirteen of us lived in the house including my mother and father. My parents had six boys and five girls. Our first house was rather small, so two of my sisters lived with my grandmother until they were nearly teenagers. I never knew my grandfather on my mother's side; he passed away before I was born. My two sisters were company for my grandmother during those years. When we eventually moved into a much larger house, we were all together again, including my grandmother. We grew up with a strong sense of family and those values are still a vital part of all of our lives. Of course in a family of this magnitude we had our share of disagreements. We were not allowed to fight and argue, but a few fights did break out over the years between us children. When we became adults we put away childish things and rallied around one another. To this day we don't believe in fighting one another and have made a pact not to allow it ever.

We still have family gatherings with all of the grandparents and great-grandparents as part of our family fellowship. My mother just passed away in February 2005, but she will always be a part of any future family gatherings. I will always cherish my memories of a good family. I can't imagine having it any better than what I've experienced from childhood up until now. When I look at a lot of the hurting families today, my heart goes out to them because the things that many of them are experiencing are foreign to me.

Believe it or not, the primary problem with children in our society is their parents. My ninth grade math teacher would always say that the reason we students weren't behaving in school was that our parents weren't maintaining our behavior at home. At the time, I was not inclined to agree with her statement, but as I got older I understood exactly what she meant. Keep your family bond strong at all cost. After all is said and done, family is usually all you have left.

Mother/Daughter

As I said in the introduction, I grew up in a house with eight females, so I have personal experience with what I am telling you in this book. The relationship between a mother and her daughter can be either the best or the worst of all family relationships. Simply because women are designed by God to relate through emotions, there is a constant struggle for the mother to let her daughter become a woman. And the daughter's battle is in allowing her mother to be the mom, even though she is now a full-grown woman herself. I cannot explain all of the dynamics going on inside the people involved because I am not a woman, so I am talking strictly from what I have seen firsthand.

My mother, who is now resting in the arms of her heavenly Father, was diligent up until her death in mothering her daughters. I don't think she ever noticed that they were grown women. She would see to it that they had the material things that may have been lacking here and there. All of the girls have many items in their homes that Mom gave to them. They didn't necessarily need all of the things that she gave to them, but this was her way of showing her love and that she was still Mom. I remember one of my sisters telling us about an incident that happened long after she got married and was living in her own home. She was home on a trip from New York where she had lived for many years. This particular day she and Mom had one of those mother/daughter moments where Mom was trying to tell her what she expected from her, even though she was on her own and married. When my sister did not respond quite the way my mother expected her to, Mom reminded her that she was still the mother and if she did not mind her manners, Mom would still whip her. Of course my sister thought it was funny and she simply laughed it off, but Mom was serious.

Mom and the girls had a very strong bond and this was the glue that kept our family strong. Simply speaking, a true mother will always be a mom to her daughters. She tries very hard to adjust when the daughters get married and go away, but the heartstrings of a real mom cannot be severed. They will just adapt to whatever it takes to keep the family together. I watched a special on television once about how the lioness works to keep the pride strong. Her sole responsibility is to make sure that the young lions are well-fed and safe from any danger. She will defend the pride with her life because her instincts compel her. Even when the male lion is out for days away from the pride, Mom never allows the cubs to leave her sight. This is a God-given trait common to humans and animals. If I had to speak for the daughters I would say, "Mothers, don't let your emotions cause you to push us away when we don't always do things your way, especially if we are grown and on our own." If I had to speak for the mothers I would say, "Daughters, you know we love you and would do anything in the world for you, but we will be your mothers for life, so just deal with it."

Mothers who disagree with many of the things that were done by their moms usually wind up doing many of the same things to their daughters. I don't mean for this to be taken the wrong way. I don't think any mother should abuse her daughter in any way. Perhaps this is what it may feel like to the young daughter, but as she gets older, she should learn to overlook the petty things her mom may do and take it all for love.

Men are not generally as emotional as women because they have been designed slightly different. As men, we expect our women to build a strong bond with the children, especially the females. It is a proven fact that children who are well-connected at home are ten times less likely to get caught up in many of the vices that are destroying our young generation today.

Daughters generally get their values from their mom, and if the mother/daughter circle closes, the enemy will not have any room to come in and divide you. Always keep in mind that family is the first church to which your daughters will ever be exposed. If they get the right training at home, they can then pass these values along to their daughters and nieces, who in turn will keep the cycle going for generations to come.

If you grew up in a dysfunctional family, you can still learn these values if you are planted in a good ministry that knows these values. This is why it is so important for church leadership to be plugged in to the spirit of God who teaches these principles. Too many people are sidetracked by a lot of glamour, though the substance of true relationship is missing. Church leadership must keep a profile of humility so that the flock can feed off of the leaders. The church should be nothing more than an extended family, teaching those same values that are practiced in the home.

Sister, Sister

As a woman of God, your love for Him should be witnessed by those who are closest to you. It is downright hypocritical for people to put on airs in public around other people and be estranged from their family members. The enemy has always fought to break up families and because women are so passionate and emotional, the devil will use those emotions to keep you apart from your family members if you're not careful. Well-meaning and loving people can become sidetracked by trivial issues that will drive a wedge between them that can last for years. Martha became very angry with Mary because she chose to minister to Jesus while Martha was more concerned with serving tables.

> And she had a sister called Mary, which also sat at Jesus' feet, and heard his word. But Martha was cumbered about much serving, and came to him, and said, Lord, dost thou not care that my sister hath left me to serve alone? bid her therefore that she help me. And Jesus answered and said unto her, Martha, Martha, thou art careful and troubled about many things: But one thing is needful: and Mary hath chosen that good part, which shall not be taken away from her.
>
> —Luke 10:39–42

This is a classic example of what can happen between biological and spiritual sisters. Don't play into the hands of the devil by letting him divide you from your loved ones. You have much to gain by keeping the family bond strong, so do all you can to maintain your sister-sister relationship.

Your relationship with your church or spiritual sister should be as strong or stronger than your relationship with your biological sister. The spiritual transformation that has taken place in you should be the same process that the sisters in your church family have experienced. You must always keep in mind that we are in a spiritual battle, and your sisters are not your enemy. When things are not going well, the devil would like you to blame your sisters, but an intelligent and well-grounded saint knows that our warfare is not carnal but spiritual. This is why the apostle Paul wrote these words to the church at Ephesus:

> For we wrestle not against flesh and blood, but against principalities, against powers, against the rulers of the darkness of this world, against spiritual wickedness in high places.
> —Ephesians 6:12

You must take care of one another and see to it that your motives are not selfish when it comes to those petty issues that divide you. I know there will be times when you have to confront issues, and you should, but once you have talked them over, let them be over. Life is too short and time is too precious to allow your unchecked emotions to destroy the time you have left on Earth.

Why We Disagree

It is perfectly okay and normal for sisters to disagree. No two people will see eye-to-eye on every issue, every time. If two people are thinking the same thing all the time, one of them has no need to be alive. We were all created with our unique, idiosyncratic ways of doing things because this is the way the Father purposed it. To disagree is normal and even healthy, but to be constantly bickering and disagreeable is devilish. You must learn how to keep your flesh in check and not allow a whole lot of drama to obstruct your view. Just look around you; there are children, sons, daughters, nieces, nephews, and a host of other people who need you to be stable for their sakes. You cannot pass much value on if all you have is a lot of drama going on in your life. When you have a disagreement, sit down at a convenient time, sooner rather than later, and put all of the issues on the table. Allow each person to talk out their frustration without being interrupted. Once this has happened, come to a consensus as to what should be done about the issues at hand. When this is complete, hold hands and pray for the situation and one another immediately. Vow never again to allow any issues to go unchecked between you.

If for some reason you cannot get to this point with one another, you must bring in a neutral party who is willing to mediate between the two of you. Repeat the same steps with the mediator present and allow him or her to call the shots. Keep in mind that the mediator is only there because you could not do this on your own, so you cannot attack the mediator when the decision is made. If after this point the two of you are still not getting things together, somebody is either not being totally honest or being selfish about the situation. Jesus left a methodology in Matthew 18:15–16 for us to resolve disputes: "If a brother sins against you, go to him privately and confront him with his fault. If he listens and confesses it, you have won back a brother. But if not, then take one or two others with you and go back to him again, proving everything you say by these witnesses" (TLB).

Due to our fallen nature, it is really hard for us to understand the concept of unconditional love, but God commands us to practice it. Sometimes we hurt those who are closest to us the most because we have not yet learned how to handle people we don't understand or disagree with. You have been called to live peacefully with all men. These are kingdom principles that are designed to keep the enemy from dividing and conquering us as a family of believers.

Sharing Our Dreams

Remember when you were a little girl? You had such high hopes and dreams. You spent time with other girls and talked about boys, dressed in your special attire, put on your favorite makeup, and of course, did your hair perfectly. This kind of loving and friendly exchange goes on among young girls even today. Now that you are women and have become more mature and responsible, these dreams can become your reality. When I say dreams, I don't mean your childhood fantasies; I mean the fellowship with your friends that made your childhood so great. You can and should continue to talk to one another often about the things that you love and enjoy. As sisters and as a family, your life together here on Earth should be filled with pleasant memories of one another. It would be a tragedy to let your years slip by and have nothing to show for your relationships but broken dreams. Your family may be all that you have and if you cannot share your dreams with them, you will be out in the cold.

If for some reason you did not have the advantage of being raised in a home where these types of values were shared, it is not too late. You can start from where you are and begin to build the kind of ties that will establish a legacy for the next generation. To have broken dreams is one thing, but to not dream at all is unthinkable. Everything that has happened to you in your past was designed to prepare you for the person you are to become. Your biological parents were given the responsibility of birthing you into this world, but your future is not in their control. Breath and life was given to you by God–not your parents. Even if as a child you missed out on the opportunity to dream, it is not over. The fact that you have made it to this place in life and have the privilege of connecting with groups like Destiny means that God is trying to show you just how much He is in charge of your life. He has only great things in store for your future. Listen to what the prophet wrote about you in Jeremiah 29:12–14: "'In those days when you pray, I will listen. If you look for me in earnest, you will find me when you seek me. I will be found by you,' says the LORD. 'I will end your captivity and restore your fortunes. I will gather you out of the nations where I sent you and bring you home again to your own land'" (NLT). God gave these words to the nation of Israel over twenty-five hundred years ago. His commitment to you is no different today. When you understand who you are in God, never again will Satan be able to control you with your past. And the next time he tries to remind of your past, you remind him of his future.

I Still Love You

When it's all over at the end of the day, everybody wants to hear these words. Families must learn the power of these words. Of course the words must carry some weight and not just roll off our lips as empty rhetoric. When you say, "I love you," every action should back up your words. If there was an issue in the family that created a little turmoil, or maybe a lot, true family knows how to come together, put the issues on the table, and rationally resolve them. People should not walk away feeling like they have just escaped from a bear cage. Somebody must have a degree of wisdom to bring the family together for the purpose of working out those tough issues that will find their way into even the best of families.

No one is exempt from the attack of the devil. The greater the family, the stronger the attack will be. Study the Book of Job; in the first five chapters you will see that God permitted the devil to strike Job's life. Even Job's wife did not understand what was going on. Job knew enough about the love of God to hold his head up through the storm. If you read it all, you will see that the storm did not last forever. As severe as it was, Job won the battle, and you can too if you know your true enemy. It is not your mother or your daughter; Satan is throwing the rock and hiding his hands. If you are not careful, you will allow him to use you to inflict harm on your precious loved ones and when it is over, you will be hurt the most. Learn how to say the words, "I love you,"—as well as, "I'm sorry," "Excuse me," "Thank you," "Please," "Forgive me," and "Have a nice day"—and you will feel better about yourself.

When Jesus taught His disciples to pray, "Thy will be done in earth, as it in heaven" (Matt. 6:10), He was teaching a principle that is not natural but supernatural. In heaven, there is no hatred, dissention, lust, envy, or any of the emotional strongholds that we struggle with here in the flesh. As we come to better understand the principles of the kingdom and grow stronger in our spirit, we will be able to overcome those weaknesses that sow division among us. All of the fighting that exists in families and other groups is nothing but the struggle of our weak flesh. Galatians 5:19–21 defines every area of our physical struggles. Study these terms individually and master them in your life. If you can do this in your life, you will never again have a problem with loving others.

The Superior Woman's Challenge for Chapter 2

1. If you have a strong family already, begin to think of ways to make it even stronger. Study the lives of other strong families through books, family reunions, etc.

2. If you do not have a strong family, start from where you are, within yourself, and seek God's guidance in building a strong relationship with other family members.

3. If your family members overall are not God-fearing and loving people, it may be hard to relate to them but try to find ways to do so.

4. If you have a good relationship with your mother, you should do all you can to let her know how much you appreciate this relationship; after all, many people do not have it.

5. If you have a strained relationship with your mother, begin to work on things that you can change within yourself to make the relationship better. Give her the benefit of the doubt.

6. Sisters should be the best of friends, but often they behave like enemies. Avoid this by loving your sister unconditionally.

7. Sometimes family members will carry around unresolved issues for years, not even speaking to one another. As a woman of character and purpose, do not let the devil cause you to display this type of attitude; it is ungodly and ugly. You must let your inner beauty show at all times.

Journal

Use this section to log special events (i.e., spiritual breakthroughs, special messages, meeting of new friends, etc.).

Week 1

_____
_____
_____
_____
_____
_____

Week 2

_____
_____
_____
_____
_____
_____

Week 3

Week 4

Closing

The aged women likewise, that they be in behaviour as becometh holiness, not false accusers, not given to much wine, teachers of good things; That they may teach the young women to be sober, to love their husbands, to love their children, To be discreet, chaste, keepers at home, good, obedient to their own husbands, that the word of God be not blasphemed.

—Titus 2:3–5

Chapter 3

Mother Knows Best

> It is the instinct, intuition, impulse, insight, love, compassion, sympathy, empathy, consideration, care, understanding, and the need to nurture in you that causes you to know best when it comes to your children.

THE MATERNAL TIES BETWEEN a mother and her child create a bond that is usually unlike anything else a child will ever experience in life. To a child, Mom is larger than life. In this context, I am assuming that the mother has built a good relationship with the child. Children should grow up loving both parents, but mothers have an advantage. The bond that mothers hold should never create any type of jealousy by the father but serve to make the family bond stronger. In the eyes of the child, Mother knows best because she is usually there most of the time taking care of the intimate needs of her children. A good mother will never use this tie as an advantage to dampen the child's relationship with the father. It is so unfortunate but many women will use the child as a pawn in the spousal relationship when things are not going well. Understanding mothers should learn how to deal with their issues as adults and never bring the children in when the relationship between her and the children's father may not be going so well.

As a mother, your child is going to believe in you because this is the way God has designed it to be. The greatest things that a mother can do for her children are to love them and to build their faith in God. Since her influence will supersede the father in many ways, the success of the formative years of the child will be credited to her for the most part. This time should be given to the proper training that you can find in the children's book in the Destiny 200 and Beyond Family Series.

The way a child relates to his father, siblings, and other close associates will have much to do with the type of values he learns. Your relationship with God depends on the success you have when raising your children. God is depending on you to provide a moral foundation for your offspring. Proverbs 22:6 commands, "Train up a child in the way he should go: and when he is old, he will not depart from it." Training a child is two-dimensional; it involves both precept and example. Telling a child what to do is only half of the battle in raising healthy and happy children. One of the biggest mistakes that many parents make is forcing their values on the child. It does not matter how well your intentions are or how good the information is that you are trying to convey, if you do not live these values in your own life, it will not work for the child. Except in rare cases, children usually follow parents who have a strong bond with them.

As a mother, you should have a strategy on how to train your children in the ways of the Lord. I am intentionally leaving the father's role out in this segment because this book is about women. I do know that his role is important in order to bring balance into the child's life. Take it upon yourself to instill all that you can in your children so as to pass on your legacy into their lives. No one can take the place of a mom except a better mom. It you intend to hear the words, "Mother knows best," start during prenatal care.

Nurturer

A nurturer is tantamount to a nurse, which is someone who cares, looks after, harbors, and supports people. You will even have to play the literal role of a nurse many times over. Over the years I watched my children's mom give them the intense care that is frequently needed in raising children. Those sudden colds, earaches, nose bleeds, and countless other things that can happen in the life of a growing child are usually noticed initially by the mother. Even if the father has noticed the need first, he generally passes this job on to the mother. Don't feel like the father does not care when he does this; he just knows that you are usually better than him at nurturing in this way. In 2 Kings 4:19 you can see the validity of my story being played out over twenty-five hundred years ago. "And he said unto his father, My head, my head. And he said to a lad, Carry him to his mother." The father in this story knew that the child's mother should be called upon when a true nurturer was needed. This story captures the essence of a mother's heart when it comes to her offspring. She was tenacious and adamant about getting help for her son. Though at first the husband did not know the gravity of the child's injury, the mother would not relent.

As a mother, you have the distinct role of completing your mate when it comes to the children. The nature and instincts that you were given place you at an advantage when it comes to picking up on the needs of the children. By no means does this diminish or take anything away from the father. His instincts as they relate to the family comprise a different aspect altogether. The two of you working in the life of the child for his or her good is what constitutes good parenting. Allow these different roles to play out in their natural order and you will raise healthy and happy children. The husband should not take this maternal bond between the mother and child as a threat to his authority in the home.

Always remember that a good family is one that has the spiritual hierarchy functioning properly. This structure has been put in place for the sake of order. Use your nurturing instinct to build your children's emotional strength. Love and tenderness is passed on to children by the way they are handled by their parents. Children who have not been given the nurturing touch that generally comes from the mother tend to grow up cold and hardened. As I watch my wife daily using this strong nurturing instinct to raise our children, it makes me feel like the happiest man in the world. As much as I love my children, I know that I do not possess many of those qualities when it comes to children. I am prone to discipline and putting in structure while she pours in the nurturing and compassion. This is how a relationship should function. Husband and wife are supposed to complete one another, not compete with one another.

Teacher

The mother is a child's first teacher for the same reason she is a nurturer. I remember when I was probably no more than five or six years old that I made fun of an old man who was extremely impoverished. He lived in a little hut that was about one hundred square feet at most. It was actually dug into the ground about three feet. This particular day as we were riding by his house, I began to laugh and make fun of the living conditions of this man. Immediately after I made my condescending remarks, my mom began to chastise me about my attitude towards this old man.

It was in these formative years of my siblings and I that our mother taught us morals and values that would last a lifetime. Teaching our children at an early age is what it's going to take to get the next generation right with God. The Bible says in Proverbs 22:15, "Foolishness is bound in the heart of a child; but the rod of correction shall drive it far from him." When a child is corrected by good teaching from loving parents, he will surely achieve success.

I said something in one of the previous segments that merits repeating. Teaching is two-dimensional; it involves both precepts and example. When you are teaching your children, academic schooling accounts for part of the child's education, but morals and values must be taught by demonstration and example. There are many parents who use profane language, smoke, drink alcohol, and even expose their children to sexually explicit materials. Some even expose them to their own sexual escapades and think nothing of it. Of course, the godly mother knows how to teach her children good biblical principles that will give them the moral foundation that is required to live a wholesome life. Use your motherly wit to teach your children every day. Moses left instructions for parents nearly three thousand years ago in Deuteronomy 11:18–19: "Therefore shall ye lay up these my words in your heart and in your soul, and bind them for a sign upon your hand, that they may be as frontlets between your eyes. And ye shall teach them your children, speaking of them when thou sittest in thine house, and when thou walkest by the way, when thou liest down, and when thou risest up."

Teaching her children should be the primary role of a mother. The formative years of a child's life are usually dominated by the mother. This is a privilege as well as a responsibility that cannot be underestimated. God is going to hold mothers responsible for the stewardship commitment that was assigned to their hands. Use every minute of your time wisely, teach by precept and by example and God will reward you.

Counselor

Good counsel is what every child needs when they have lost their way or simply need to be focused in the right direction. Once again, due to the maternal ties, the mother is usually the first one the child confides in for consolation. John Maxwell, a noted author, says leadership is nothing more than having influence. The term *influence* means pouring of fluid. In essence, as a counselor, you are pouring in the fluid of advice and guidance that will help focus your children towards their future. You can keep them from making some of the mistakes that you had to learn from as a younger person. I remember when I was about sixteen years of age my dad sent me on a job to work with his tractor. During the course of the day, the tractor ran out of oil and the engine burned up. Dad became very upset about this because he thought that I should have known to check the oil. As a means of punishment, he decided to cut my pay and use the money to repair the tractor. Needless to say, I was not a happy camper. I went to my mom to talk about this issue because I knew she would listen to my side. Even though she never went against my father's decision, I was satisfied knowing that I could talk to her about this issue. I tell this story all the time even though it was thirty-five years ago because it was the catalyst for changing my life. I went away to the military still angry with my father about this whole issue, and it was the turning point in my life. My mom never agreed or disagreed with my dad's decision, but she gave me the consolation that was needed to move on in spite of the issue.

Now that I'm a man with six children of my own, my wife will sometimes do the same things with my children that my mom did for me. She has to occasionally interpret my intentions to the children so they will know that I'm not out to hurt them even though my decisions may be a little harsh. This is how a good family is supposed to work. It takes the mother to balance the father and the father to balance the mother. When mom gives godly council to her children, it serves to anchor the children to the home when the sea of life gets a little rough. From time to time your motherly wit as a counselor must be used to soothe the spirit of your children. The devil is waiting to lure them away from the values that you are trying to instill in them, so be vigilant and on your post to watch for the souls of your children, which God has entrusted to you. The term *counsel* means to guide, direct, instruct, advise, recommend, and encourage—all of which a good mother will gladly do to and for her children. This may not always be an easy thing, but it will always be rewarding. God will not forget your work of faith and labor of love for His inheritance.

The Housewife

In our modern era, the role of housewife has basically become a thing of the past. Many women would be insulted if you referred to them by this term. With the rising cost of living and our constant quest for more material things, it is almost impossible to run a house on only one income. But in spite of both parents working, mothers usually wind up doing the lion's share of the housework.

For the past fifteen years of my life, I have become more aware of the responsibility of housework. With the transition of my vocation, it affords me a lot more time to be in the home and boy, do I see firsthand that it is no picnic maintaining a house, especially when you have a house full of children. On average, women still handle the everyday issues around the home more than men. I am probably one of the exceptions as I do a lot of housework because my taste for housecleaning is on a different level than my spouse. This is by no means a derogatory statement towards her. On the other hand, I cannot hold a candle to her when it comes to the many things that she does to keep our home stable. Our children are her number one concern and this is where she puts most of her energy when it comes to the home. She works an outside job and it would be totally selfish for me to put all of the work on her. Together, we balance the load of raising the children, keeping the house in order, and maintaining a standard of living that we both enjoy. All of our needs are met, and we enjoy the home God has blessed us with.

If you are a typical housewife, don't become bitter if you seem to be overloaded at times because this is probably the norm in the average house. Finding grace in all that you do is the only lasting consolation you are going to get in this life. If your spouse does not give you the support that you think you deserve, I suggest that you seek counseling as a couple, but don't allow yourself to lose focus on your personal commitment to God. Sometimes you can become overwhelmed with the demands of housework, a full-time job, and handling most of the children's needs. I know that many of our men have been derelict in holding up their share of the work in these areas. The average guy who works all day will come home expecting to do nothing for the rest of the evening but watch television or fraternize with the boys. The woman, on the other hand, is left to do all of the above chores alone. This is absolutely unfair and I hope that men will begin to see this for themselves. The men's book in the Destiny 2000 and Beyond Family Series will help your husband in this area; encourage him to get the book and join a group where the series is being taught.

The Superior Woman's Challenge for Chapter 3

1. Nothing can be more rewarding for you than being a good mother. Work on your parenting skills to become the best at being a mom.

2. A child must be connected at all times to one or both parents. Never let an issue sever the ties with your children or the enemy will take over their lives.

3. Pray often for your children, touch them, hug them, tell them you love them, and do not display a bad attitude, because they will inherit it from you.

4. Being a mother is not always easy, but it is always rewarding. Seek God daily for the wisdom and patience to deal with your children individually; they are not all the same.

5. Try to spend some individual, quality time with your children on a frequent basis. It will build a bond for a lifetime.

6. As a mother, you must be extremely careful not to send the wrong message to your daughter by letting her dress inappropriately. Our culture is corrupt; do not follow the trend.

7. A mother who knows best knows that Daddy cannot be ignored; teach your children to respect their father or they will probably hate you in the long run for not doing so.

Journal

Use this section to log special events (i.e., spiritual breakthroughs, special messages, meeting of new friends, etc.).

Week 1

Week 2

Week 3

_____
_____
_____
_____
_____
_____
_____

Week 4

_____
_____
_____
_____
_____
_____
_____
_____

Peace I leave with you, my peace I give unto you: not as the world giveth, give I unto you. Let not your heart be troubled, neither let it be afraid.

—John 14:27

Chapter 4

SUFFERING FROM WITHIN

> Women who continue to allow men or anyone for that matter to abuse them—verbally, physically, or in any other manner—have not tapped into the reality of who they truly are.

W**HEN I STARTED TO** write this book for women, the subject of abuse was not on my agenda, but as I continued to seek God for the areas that needed to be addressed, I felt led to include this topic. Women who continue to allow men or anyone for that matter to abuse them—verbally, physically, or in any other manner—have not tapped into the reality of who they truly are. During this segment I will try to give you as much spiritual insight as possible to help you overcome these difficult areas in your life. I am not a clinical psychologist, so I will not be dealing with the topic of abuse from this aspect. I have seen quite a number of women who were so involved emotionally that it became almost impossible to see through the pain.

The one thing that has worked for me over the years whenever I get to a roadblock is to surrender my will to the will of God. No amount of psychological counseling is going to help a person who is not willing to look deep within and draw from their own inner strength. When a psychologist attempts to help a person solve a problem, it is usually the information that the individual gives to the doctor that is used to help them. In essence, a person who is suffering emotionally can solve their own problems if they know how to decipher their emotions.

Knowing who you are from within has everything to do with the way you choose to handle your problems. Depending on the amount of confidence you have in God, and in your own ability in Him, you can get through anything that the enemy puts in your path.

A person who eventually succumbs to abuse is usually worn down over a period of years by incidents that go unresolved. Such a process requires you to allow yourself to believe those things about yourself that the devil has planted in your spirit. When you begin to believe the lies, you will begin to live them out. If you are consistently told derogatory things about yourself, it is your choice to accept them or not. Even if the comments are true about you, you still have the option to rise above your weakness and become a better person. I can remember times when I felt a bit inferior to others because I thought they had an advantage over me. When I became fully in touch with my inner self and began to discover who I was in God, I learned not to measure myself by other people but by who I was in God. When God created you, He had no intentions of creating anyone else that was exactly like you. With this in mind, you need to diligently seek God and find out what it is that He has created you to do. Once you have done this, your entire efforts for the rest of your life should be focused upon developing yourself around your purpose. It is the lack of purpose that causes people to surrender their will to other people. Other people can have your support but only God should have your will. The human will is the strongest force there is. It is a difference in the power of their respective wills that keeps one person empowered while the other would die from the same ordeal. It takes faith in God and the faith of God in you for you to triumph in difficult times.

We are created in the image of God and God is a Spirit. When you understand that your spirit can only be empowered by spiritual things, you will know how to use Scripture and the power of faith through prayer to build your spirituality. It is the spirit of God empowering your spirit that will keep you from giving in to any outside force. Here is what the apostle Paul wants you to know about spiritual empowerment:

> Be careful for nothing; but in every thing by prayer and supplication with thanksgiving let your requests be made known unto God. And the peace of God, which passeth all understanding, shall keep your hearts and minds through Christ Jesus. Finally, brethren, whatsoever things are true, whatsoever things are honest, whatsoever things are just, whatsoever things are pure, whatsoever things are lovely, whatsoever things are of good report; if there be any virtue, and if there be any praise, think on these things.
> —Philippians 4:6–8

When you master these verses, never again will you suffer from depression or abuse of any sort.

During the remainder of your journey through this book, work through all of the exercises carefully. Allow the principles within to take root in your life. There is a lot of truth in the phrase, "Practice makes perfect." You must remember that God created you in His image. The word *image* means "likeness." God is a Spirit, and to be in His likeness means that you are a spirit also. Our culture forces us to put a lot of emphasis on physical things and knowledge, but is does not teach how to develop our spirit.

God knew exactly what you and I would need in the realm of spiritual things so He left the record of His Word to teach us faith and character. He allows us to learn through the lives of those who have gone on before us so that we will be equipped to build His kingdom. You are a part of the generation of kingdom builders and your effectiveness in this area is directly related to your understanding of the kingdom. You cannot understand kingdom principles unless you have been birthed into the kingdom. This story in the Gospel of John will shed a little light on this subject:

> There was a man of the Pharisees, named Nicodemus, a ruler of the Jews: The same came to Jesus by night, and said unto him, Rabbi, we know that thou art a teacher come from God: for no man can do these miracles that thou doest, except God be with him. Jesus answered and said unto him, Verily, verily, I say unto

thee, Except a man be born again, he cannot see the kingdom of God. Nicodemus saith unto him, How can a man be born when he is old? can he enter the second time into his mother's womb, and be born? Jesus answered, Verily, verily, I say unto thee, Except a man be born of water and of the Spirit, he cannot enter into the kingdom of God. That which is born of the flesh is flesh; and that which is born of the Spirit is spirit. Marvel not that I said unto thee, Ye must be born again. The wind bloweth where it listeth, and thou hearest the sound thereof, but canst not tell whence it cometh, and whither it goeth: so is every one that is born of the Spirit. Nicodemus answered and said unto him, How can these things be? Jesus answered and said unto him, Art thou a master of Israel, and knowest not these things?

—John 3:1–10

There are millions of people who walk through the church doors every week and are in the same predicament as Nicodemus. They have been in church all of their lives and still do not know what the kingdom of God is all about. They know a whole lot about church work but not kingdom building. Kingdom building transcends the local church and the denomination barriers that most people cannot see beyond. You will have to learn how to think outside of the box in order to learn these principles. If you are in any type of relationship that is causing you to be depressed or you are being abused physically and/or emotionally, you can begin to break free the moment you get in touch with the spiritual aspect of who you are. No amount of psychology can get you in touch with this area of your life if it is not teaching you these biblical principles. You need to have God's Spirit empowering your spirit. This spiritual infusion will set you on a course that you never thought you could obtain.

Once you know your purpose in life, it will be impossible for anybody to take that away from you. If you are trapped in a situation that seems to be insurmountable, you are at the right place for a miracle. A miracle is defined as something that is impossible to accomplish by human means. I remember going through a period when I thought that my life was finished. I was so broken inside; it took everything within me to fight my way through this struggle. I knew that God had not forsaken me, but I felt like he had dropped me into a huge body of water to teach me how to swim. I had the faith to believe and it took every bit of it to get me to the next level in my life. This is exactly how faith works. It is what you hold on to when there is nothing left to hold on to.

Suffering is redemptive if you know why you are suffering. When God allows His children to undergo suffering, it is for the purpose of bringing out the best in them. It is natural for us stay in our comfort zone, but suffering has a way of moving us from that spot. When eaglets get up in size, the mother eagle will turn up the sticks in the nest in order to coerce the little chicks to fly. If God does not allow us to suffer, we will never be able to testify of His miraculous power of deliverance. You can rise above your struggle if you will allow God to bring you out. He is waiting for you to surrender your all to Him.

Trapped

Some people are trapped between the devil and the river. Either way they turn, it doesn't look good. I want to take this moment to prophesy to you: When there is no way out, there is a way up. Up is where you need to look when you seem to be trapped in situations that look impossible to you. Every situation that you will ever become involved in has within it the solution to get you out. If you study the right material long enough, you can get out too. If you are in a relationship of any sort that has you bound, this is not God's will for your life. You have to decide whether or not you are going to give in to your surroundings or are you going to take charge and use your spiritual authority. I have seen people hold on to other people and things that they knew were literally killing them. In spite of the pain they continued to subject themselves to the same situation because they were afraid, weak, or had little or no confidence in themselves.

If you don't believe in yourself, no one else is going to believe in you either. If self-defeat is your mind-set, others may show you favor, but it would only be for their benefit to exploit you. This is the kind of world we are living in; it truly is the survival of the fittest. Now that you know this, you need to become spiritually fit to hold your own in life. Others instinctively know when they have come across a weakling and many people are waiting to lure you into their traps.

It has been said that no one can make you feel inferior unless you give them permission to do so. This is a very profound and true statement. The slave owners were able to subject many of the slaves because they had succumbed to the slave mentality. They did have a choice: submit and live or rebel and take a chance on their lives. Every individual will have to decide within themselves whether or not they are willing to submit or fight for their lives. The question that you must answer in a situation such as this is, How bad do I want to be free? If it's not worth it to you to fight for your freedom, maybe you would be better off trapped. On the other hand, if you know deep down in your heart that you are worth more than the situation that you are trapped in, you will fight your way out. It has been said that a man who is worth saving will not drown. In essence, God will not let the devil destroy you if you are woman enough to fight for your life.

If you are in an abusive relationship, you probably feel trapped. Your world can become your reality, and if this is what you believe, you are what you think. However, if you are willing to get in touch with your inner strength and put God in front, He will give you an escape route to freedom in Christ. I have heard the testimonies of those who have been up against the wall with a gun to their head, but God would not let the devil win. Not only that, I too was once in a situation where my life was threatened at gunpoint. I was told to run for my life or be shot if I didn't. After thinking about the ultimatum, I decided to hold my ground and not move. I knew that I was not guilty of any wrongdoing and running would be an admission of guilt. When I chose to hold my ground, my attacker came out and apologized for his stupidity. When you learn to call the devil's bluff under the authority of the Holy Spirit, God will give you victory.

The worst thing that can happen to you can turn out to be the best thing. When he was confronted with death, the apostle Paul wrote in Philippians 1:20–21, "According to my earnest expectation and my hope, that in nothing I shall be ashamed, but that with all boldness, as always, so now also Christ shall be magnified in my body, whether it be by life, or by death. For to me to live is Christ, and to die is gain." I want to share two other biblical stories of situations similar to yours.

When it looks as if you are trapped with nowhere to turn, this is an excellent opportunity for God to show up and show out on your behalf. Always remember these words during your toughest moment: Man's extremity becomes God's opportunity to show up on his behalf. When David and his men returned to his stronghold in Ziglaz, they found the city burned to the ground and their wives and children taken into captivity. David and his men fell on their faces and wept until there were no more tears left. David prayed to God and asked Him for direction at this point in his life. After he prayed, God gave him a word of encouragement and from that moment on, he was ready to get back in the fight (1 Samuel 30). No outside force can keep you down when you learn how to depend on God for strength.

When you are trapped by your own emotions, it can be more devastating than being behind bars. A story is told about an elephant that was tied to a tree for an extensive period of time. One day a man came by and cut the rope from the tree to set the elephant free. As he began to walk away, he noticed that the elephant was still pacing around the tree. Finally, in order to expose the elephant to freedom, the man had to physically move it away from the tree. Sometimes we can be trapped by our own thinking. The Bible declares that you are what you think. When you begin to empower your mind with positive words, you can get out of the rut of depression and bondage. Jesus came to give you abundant life. It is the devil that is causing you to feel as if you are still tied to the tree. He will keep you going around and around and around in this circle until he totally destroys your mind. If you have made it this far into this book, you still have hope. Get a hold on your emotions and build your spiritual stamina for the life ahead of you. You can make it from here if you believe in yourself and the God who gave you life.

How Do I Get Free?

Most of what we talked about in the previous segment is what it's going to take to get you free from any type of bondage or abuse. I want to further talk to you about outside support groups that are waiting to give you a hand up and out. Like the gentlemen who cut the rope from the neck of the elephant and moved him to a new environment, the support groups will guide you onto a new path. I can only point you in the direction that you need to go, I will probably never get the chance to speak to you personally. If you are currently attending a church or some type of organization that can give you the spiritual guidance needed, start there. Don't make the assumption that people should know what is going on inside of you. This is usually not the case. You need to reach out for support if you are serious about getting help. If you are in a situation with an abusive spouse, parents, or so-called friend, you will have to make it clear to your support group what you are experiencing.

Being in the presence of the right people will make all the difference in how well you will come out of your period of bondage. The group that will probably help you the most is one that has the Bible as its foundation. It does not necessarily have to be a church group but it needs to have sound principles based on the Bible. Always remember that an individual or group that is just teaching you psychology is only meeting half of the needs that must be addressed for you to become completely whole. It would also serve you well to find out a little about the people to whom you are going to entrust your life.

There are all sorts of people who are just out to get your money or to take advantage of your emotional weakness. The process of becoming free from spiritual bondages and strongholds must start with the will of the individual. When you fully decide that you want to come out of the slump you are in, other people will only be a support system to help you through. It is like having a baby—when the third trimester of pregnancy is over, the baby is going to come even if you do not have anyone around. As you already know, many women birth their own babies alone. Your primary trust needs to be in God and in your own desire to break the chains that are holding you back.

You already have the ability to be free; the question is, do you have the will? When people have subjected themselves to the will of other people for so long, they seem to lose sight of their own willingness to do for themselves. As you are reading this segment, God is putting out His hands to help you up. He created you to be free, but freedom must be your choice.

Handling Frustrations

Frustration and depression from abuse are two different emotions. The term *frustration* is defined as "aggravation, irritation, annoyance, disappointment, and dissatisfaction," all of which are basically the way we handle things as they come to us. In essence, frustration can and usually is self-inflicted. What may frustrate one person may be fun for another. When our youngest son was still sleeping in the bed with my wife and I, I could not stand to have him put his foot on me when I was trying to sleep. It seemed as if it weighed fifty pounds. My wife on the other hand, did not have a problem at all. She actually thought it was funny when I told her how I felt about it. I assume that this was natural to her since she carried him for nine months. Abuse has more to do with an outside person inflicting their will upon you; frustration has more to do with not being able to put things in perspective. It is the inability to focus on the main thing at the moment because your vision is impaired by many other things. It is like driving on the freeway in the fog—you are anticipating at any minute to run into another automobile. As a child of God, you need to know that you have access to Him at any given moment, no matter how trivial or great your issues may be. His voice during such times will come to give you focus and comfort if you choose to tune in to Him.

Sometimes before we catch ourselves, we are so far into what is confusing our minds that we forget He is near us. Our patience toward many of the things that come up in our lives will usually determine whether or not they frustrate us. Patience is a biblical virtue that you must cultivate in your life. It can be the determining factor as to where you will spend eternity. Here is what Jesus taught concerning patience in Luke 21:19, "In your patience possess ye your souls." The apostle James also gave us a word of wisdom concerning patience, "So let it grow, and don't try to squirm out of your problems. For when your patience is finally in full bloom, then you will be ready for anything, strong in character, full and complete. If you want to know what God wants you to do, ask him, and he will gladly tell you, for he is always ready to give a bountiful supply of wisdom to all who ask him; he will not resent it" (James 1:4–5, TLB).

So as you can see, as you mature in the faith, you shouldn't have to fight the battle of frustration. There will always be times when things will come upon us that are a bit confusing, but the way you respond to them will determine how much they affect you. Always remember that God's Holy Spirit is within you to give you the strength that is needed to get you through the frustrating moments of your life.

Mood Swings

Moodiness results from a combination of emotional changes and chemical fluctuation within the body. Much of the mood swings, especially the emotional aspect to it, is also related to your level of maturity. The ability to handle or control your emotions is directly related to your spiritual stability. Your emotions are actually part of your spiritual makeup, and the more you are in touch with this area of your life, the more you will be able to control your mood. The thoughts that you allow to harden into a mind-set are the ones that will set your mood for the moment. Fortunately, the apostle Peter gave us as an antidote for mood swings in 1 Peter 1:13: "Wherefore gird up the loins of your mind, be sober, and hope to the end for the grace that is to be brought unto you at the revelation of Jesus Christ." To *gird* means to control and gather your thoughts and to not let them waver. When you do not take the time to fill those empty spaces with positive words, the enemy of your soul readily takes advantage of this opening to sow thoughts of discouragement into your mind.

Another passage of Scripture that would serve you well to put into your spiritual arsenal is Philippians 4:8. "Finally, brethren, whatsoever things are true, whatsoever things are honest, whatsoever things are just, whatsoever things are pure, whatsoever things are lovely, whatsoever things are of good report; if there be any virtue, and if there be any praise, think on these things."

Chemical imbalance is also another reason for moodiness. As I was writing this book I went online to research some of the medical findings on the subject of chemical imbalances. I am certainly not a medical doctor or a psychologist, so my immediate suggestion to an individual who may have questions in this area is for them to see a specialist. I will also suggest that you read up on the topic on your own. You can go online as I did or ask a professional for books that will shed some light on this subject. One of the great disparities in the medical profession is that they do not usually make the connection between the spiritual realm and natural problems. Most psychologists will probably not suggest that you deal with your emotional issues through prayer and getting in touch with your spirituality. Medication of some sort will usually be the first advice. I do believe that the medical profession has made some tremendous inroads dealing with certain medical problems, but they have yet to give God all of the credit for their findings.

I happen to think that moodiness is basically a spiritual issue. I think that it is natural for you to have different emotional responses to different things in life, but your ability to keep your mind intact is directly related to your spiritual health. Isaiah 26:3 is my biblical reference to this matter: "He will keep in perfect peace all those who trust in him, whose thoughts turn often to the Lord!" (TLB). Meditate on these words.

The Superior Woman's Challenge for Chapter 4

1. Much of the abuse and suffering women experience from men is self-inflicted, in that they ignore the warning signs of an abusive man. Do not tolerate abuse in any form. Sever ties beforehand, and save yourself a lifetime of hell.

2. What love is to a women is not always the same thing to a man. If he tells you he loves you, the words alone mean absolutely nothing if they are not proven with deeds. Make him prove his love before you give him yours.

3. Don't ever use sex as a way to get a mate, which is equivalent to using a trap to catch a snake. You may get poisoned by a bite from which you cannot recover.

4. A man cannot abuse you unless you give him permission. When you know who you are and who you belong to, you will know how to avoid or get free from someone who abuses you. This power comes from the strength you get from God through prayer and a good relationship with other strong people.

5. A support group with biblical teachings is the best way to get out of an abusive relationship. Call the Destiny line in the back of this book if need be and we will try to help find one of these groups in your area.

6. There is no power greater than the human spirit; through it, you can conquer anything you choose with God on your side.

Journal

Use this section to log special events (i.e., spiritual breakthroughs, special messages, meeting of new friends, etc.).

Week 1

Week 2

Week 3

Week 4

But let it be the hidden man of the heart, in that which is not corruptible, even the ornament of a meek and quiet spirit, which is in the sight of God of great price.

—1 Peter 3:44

Chapter 5

It's the Lady in You

> Femininity is the lady in you, the side that wants to be cuddled, needed, wanted, loved, and made to feel special; it is the essence of who you are.

I grew up in a house with a mother, grandmother, five sisters, and one step-sister. I was always around a host of female aunts, cousins, church sisters, and ultimately, many nieces. The one thing that they all had in common was that they wanted to know if they looked good to the guys? I've seen women who try to play the hard role but this is not what they are deep down inside. It's a façade or veneer that is put up for various reasons but they really want the same things as other women. Every woman wants to get in touch with her feminine side, with the lady in herself. When God created Eve, she was taken directly from the inside of Adam. He created them equally but with different roles. The differences that are revealed in their separate roles were designed to compliment each other. The desire that a woman has for a man is just the natural side of her wanting to connect with her place of origin. As a woman, you should not hide the femininity that is in you by trying to be hard when it comes to men. You are at your best when you display kindness, love, passion, and your sexuality. Looks account for only a part of feminine sexuality; the way your feel about yourself is the remaining part. Smiling often and being transparent makes women appealing to men. I'm not suggesting that you become a flirt just to attract the attention of men. In my opinion, a flirt is a person who sets out just to bring attention to himself or herself. This is why so many women dress provocatively and use all sorts of jests to allure men. God frowns upon this devilish type of behavior. When you learn how to get in touch with your true feelings, natural and unrehearsed, it will be sufficient.

Much of our culture has degraded women for far too long, and many women do not know how to carry themselves when it comes to men. Let me tell you what I feel like when I come face-to-face with a woman who is flirtatious. I immediately begin to think that she thinks I am a weak, desperate guy who is looking for her to come and rescue me. Women who display this type of personality are usually domineering and controlling. Real men do not enjoy this type of behavior. When you are advertising yourself in a subtle way, it may very well attract men to you, but they will be the type of guy that only wants you for the night, or one who is passive and will not stand up and be a responsible man.

When you look at the behavior of children, girls in particular, they just want to make the connection of friendship and enjoy the moment with the boys. They have not yet learned the tricks and seductive ways that some women use to get a man's attention. If you can remember the simple innocence that you had as a child, this should be sufficient for your femininity and sexuality to surface. In the next few segments, I want to talk about some things that my wife enjoys when I make the effort to do them for her. This may not be exactly what every single woman wants, but I think that it speaks to what the majority desire from men or their spouses.

Opening the Door

The idea of opening the door for women simply suggests that you are putting her ahead of yourself. It signifies that you want her to feel special. After all, special is what she is. Sometimes I forget, or I may just elect not to do it every time, but she doesn't make a big deal out of it. Some women will force a man to do things for them and if he doesn't, a big fight ensues. This is not ladylike. If you want your husband or friend to accommodate you in this manner, use your loving feminine side to influence his behavior. Your meek tone of voice will get his attention if he is a gentleman. You must keep in mind that there is no school for men to attend to learn all of the little things that women like; you may have to be his teacher. When you are trying to teach your man in these areas, you have to be subtle about it, not letting him know that you are out to train him. The male ego is very fragile and many men frown at the very idea that a woman is trying to instruct him, especially in a forceful way. You can accomplish the job only if you skillfully use your feminine appeal.

Most men will go out of their way to do nice things for a woman because they want to be accepted by her. A man needs you in his life just as much as you desire to have him. If you are in a relationship with a person who does not want to make you feel special, you are in the wrong relationship. On the other hand, you don't want to make everything in the relationship revolve around you. All good relationships must have balance when is comes to the mutual desires to make one another happy. If you expect your mate to open the door for you, you must be willing to learn what it takes to make him feel equally special. I love it when my wife occasionally gives me a card expressing how much she loves me. I love it when she does not leave me guessing about what she wants. I also love the fact that she is not petty and she doesn't go around all day pouting about something that happened yesterday or the day before. If we encounter an issue during the course of a day, she immediately brings that issue to my attention and we talk about it. When we talk about the issue, we normally resolve it then and there rather than allow the devil to frustrate us for days and weeks to come.

Just remember that opening doors is a choice, and you want your mate to open the door out of his own free will. In order for him to want to do this, you need to remain feminine and ladylike at all times. Don't forget to remind him in a loving way about the things that you don't like, but don't be overbearing about petty issues; communicate your desires often.

Dinner and a Movie

Spending time alone with the love of your life is the best thing about a marriage. When the two of you are together and away from the distractions of the children and other daily issues that take away from your quality time, it feels like heaven. This time alone together should really be special to the both of you. If you are not married as of yet, and you are dating a special friend, you too can take advantage of a special evening such as this. This is a practice that my wife and I do each week. I set out to make it a special evening even though I usually ask her where she wants to go. Her eating habits and taste buds are different from mine, so I try to accommodate her most of the time by letting her choose the place. She is a connoisseur when it comes to tasting food. I told her that God gave women more taste buds because they really have a knack for tasting food. When we go out to eat, the taste is not as important to me, because I don't usually taste what she does. Don't get me wrong; I like the taste of good food; I'm just not as good as her when it comes to tasting certain spices and herbs.

We use the time alone to catch up on the things that we missed while we were away from each other all day. Our respective tastes in movies are about as different as our tastes in food. I like a drama here and there, but I'm more into comedy, the daily news, and of course, television ministries. I can sit and watch the news for hours, but she is only interested in the day's weather and various sitcoms. This is how she knows how to dress the kids for the day. Most of the time when we go to the movies, if it is not really capturing my attention, I will fall asleep. I already know that this in not good, but give me an E for effort. Recently we started watching movies on our home theater which gives us the same movie effect—but it does not make up for the time alone unless we are in our bedroom. Our bedroom is extremely large—eleven hundred square feet to be exact—so I can set the home theater up in the room when we want to get away from the kids. I will sometimes lock the door, if you know what I mean. This special time is precious to both of us, but being the type of mother she is, our children dominate her attention most of the time. When I lock the door, this is my way of saying that I want her all to myself. We enjoy each other in this manner because God has given us a special relationship. I would like to take this time to tell you about the marriage journal in the Destiny 2000 and Beyond Family Series so that you and your spouse can hear the whole story on building a strong relationship.

In Touch With Her Sexuality

I said in one of my previous segments that sexuality has as much to do with the way you feel as with what you look like to yourself. I want to make this clear, because beauty is in the eye of the beholder. The person who considers you to be beautiful is judging from what they see. When you look at yourself, you should see your beauty based on what you are more so than what you look like. The wise King Solomon wrote about beauty in Proverbs 31:30, "Favour is deceitful, and beauty is vain: but a woman that feareth the LORD, she shall be praised." I have seen the prettiest faces spoiled because of bad attitudes. Being sexy has more to do with your perception of who you are than with what others think of you. Most women only need to get in touch with their feminine side in order to display their sexuality. I want to make it clear once again that being sexy has little to do with being pretty. It really disgusts me when I see women who go to extremes to make up their faces and overdo their hair, thinking that this will somehow give them sex appeal. As I said before, when you go to such drastic measures to attract men, you will probably attract the wrong type. I am so sorry that our culture overall does not have a way to teach women how to adorn themselves. Jezebel in the Bible got a bad rap because she painted her hair and displayed a spirit of control over her husband King Ahab. If you don't want to be associated with her, check out your apparel by getting the opinion of someone who has good values, and loves you enough to tell you the truth about how you look. I am not at all against makeup but I have a problem with women who don't seem to know how much to put on. Here is my take on the subject: if the makeup is not even with your skin tone, you may need a little professional help.

Being sexy does not mean being seductive, and I think that this is what some women don't understand. Seduction is a moral failure because it forces you to be deceitful. To be deceitful is to portray yourself as something that you are not. If you set out solely to convince someone that you are something you really aren't, when they find who you really are, do you think they will want to stay with you? The answer is no. Let your sexuality be natural, just the way God created you. When He made you, you were unique in His sight. And it was not your looks that He wanted to use in order to use your life. Your beauty and sexuality have everything to do with your purpose in life. Your goal is not to have everybody discover your sexuality—only the one God has for you. Here is what he promises you in Psalms 149:4: "For the LORD taketh pleasure in his people: he will beautify the meek with salvation."

How Do I Look in This?

How you look in the clothing that you wear is just as important as what your face looks like in the clothing. Once again, our culture overall is very liberal as to what it will tolerate when it comes to the way many women dress. I can only speak from my personal taste for women and clothing, and I am probably what you would call very conservative in this area. I wholeheartedly believe in what I teach the women in our ministry on this subject. I grew up in an environment that was extremely to the left with female clothing, but my years of traveling and the wisdom I've learned over the years has tempered me somewhat. As a woman of God, or one who is trying to pass godly values on to your daughters, you have to be very conscious and cautious about the message you send through your clothing. Your clothes should not be sexually revealing in any way to anyone but your husband. When I see women dressed in attire that is advertising and accentuating every part of their bodies, it tells me one of two things: either they do not know the message they are sending, or they are deliberately trying to seduce men. I can tell you firsthand of an experience that I had with a young lady who visited my house— she was married, by the way. She was wearing spandex that was very tight and revealed those parts of her body that readily captured my eyes. I then asked her why women wear their pants so tight. She said, "We want the men to look but not touch." I don't need to say anymore on this subject.

Let me just tell you that you can be sexy, feminine, and ladylike without exposing your special parts to men or women. If I can literally see your breasts, the cut is too low. If when you sit down, you have to cover up your legs to keep from exposing your thighs, the dress is too short. If the pants you are wearing reveal your shape, they are too tight. I love a woman who dresses conservatively in that the clothing is beautiful and compliments her personality. If the clothes that you wear are all together modest but your personality and character is off-center, the dress does not help. When you get in touch with your inner beauty and compliment it with beautiful clothing that covers your beautiful body, you can become a beauty queen. Our society is filled with bad models to lead our young women astray. What we need are people like you to be assertive and let your godly beauty as well as your outer beauty be exposed to this world. Our society can be no better than the models that they are exposed to every day. As a married or single woman, God is depending on you to hold up the light. Dress to impress but not provocatively; you are representing heaven.

The Superior Woman's Challenge for Chapter 5

1. When you smile, you show your personality; when you love, you show your true character. The lady in you is the two put together.

2. Sexiness is not a look but an attitude. When you master a pleasant attitude, your sexuality cannot be hidden.

3. A man may be attracted to you for a thousand reasons, but they will love you for only one reason—the lady in you.

4. Do not hesitate to tell your mate what makes you happy; he is not a mind reader, but do not nag him to do it, or he will resent you. Persuade him to do it through your ladylike charm.

5. A woman who uses makeup is one who understands the necessity of being appealing, but a woman who does not know how to use it is uninformed or confused.

6. Your clothing says a lot about you; it will even say, "I am desperate." Don't advertise your body, but display your inner beauty, which is the lady in you.

7. The lady in you is the lover in you; without the love, you will become fickle, callous, cold, and hard to deal with. Get in touch with your inner beauty; it is hidden under the pain of your past. Rid yourself of the issues and, like the sun coming over the horizon, you will shine again.

Journal

Use this section to log special events (i.e., spiritual breakthroughs, special messages, meeting of new friends, etc.).

Week 1

_____
_____
_____
_____
_____
_____
_____

Week 2

_____
_____
_____
_____
_____
_____
_____

Week 3

Week 4

*A friend loveth at all times, and
a brother is born for adversity.*

—Proverbs 17:17

Chapter 6

My Girlfriends

An acquaintance is for a season, but friendship is for a lifetime. The fact that she is a friend for life is what makes a girlfriend so special.

I'm no girl, and definitely not an expert on women, but the experience that I do have, along with what I have learned from the women that are closest to me, gives me the insight to talk about this topic. A girlfriend should be a friend that will help you to become better at life than what you are. She is a companion whose relationship with you should be complimenting and enriching in every way. You want to be able to have a few laughs with her, but you also want her to be someone who can help you deal with serious life issues. The last thing you want to do is hook up with an angry, gossiping, men-hating, disgruntled female. Whether you are married or unmarried, you do not need girlfriends who have issues with men because they will destroy your chance of ever having a good relationship with a man. Some men are dogs with a capital D, but there are still a lot of good men in the world. I know because I am one of them and I can point you to some good ones if you listen to my tips.

A girlfriend is someone who you can spend some quality time with and the two of you can benefit from the strengths and weaknesses of one another. But if you are married, your girlfriend should never, I say never, come before your husband. Your husband should not be your only friend, but he should be your best friend. If your girlfriend is not friends with your husband, sever your ties with her. She cannot be close friends with your husband, because this crosses the line of good ethics, but neither can she be his enemy. There are some women who claim to be your friend but talk badly about your husband. You need to be careful about this kind of friend; she might be trying to divide you up so she can ease her way in.

Check out your girlfriends closely, and don't close your eyes to any woman; she is flesh and all flesh can succumb to weakness at any given time. It could be innocent in the beginning, but things happen, and when they do, it can really be devastating. I'm not trying to frighten you away from your girlfriend, but what I am saying is this: your girlfriend, your boyfriend, and even your enemy can all be used by the devil, so be watchful at all times and make God your ultimate friend. He is the Friend that will stick closer than anyone you will ever meet on Earth. Good people sometimes do bad things, and you need to be aware of this at all times. "And one shall say unto him, What are these wounds in thine hands? Then he shall answer, Those with which I was wounded in the house of my friends" (Zechariah 13:6). This scripture depicts the very essence of the point I want to convey concerning some friends. A friend can hurt you more than an enemy. You would not feel betrayed if your enemy hurt you because you would have expected it. But when someone you have laughed with, cried with, and shared your innermost secrets with is the one who puts the dagger in your back, it can destroy you.

I Can Trust You

You can trust your true girlfriend to give you what you will not get from most people you know. You can expect her to be there for you when you want to just talk about the weather. She will be the one you can call on to give you a ride when you are stranded. Girlfriends will loan you money and will surely look after you when you become ill. In every area of your life, girlfriends will be there, and that's the way it should be.

When a person says "I will trust you with my life," those are very strong words, but they usually don't mean it. It is hard to say what a person will do until the very moment when it happens, but I don't know of anyone who will do this. Jesus gave his life for us once and I cannot think of a reason for me to give my life for anyone else. (I'm just keeping it real when I say this.) There is only so much trust that you can put in another human being. I find that people usually do what is most beneficial for themselves in a time of crisis. If you are on their agenda during this time, maybe you will be factored in; if not, God only knows what they will do.

You can trust a friend to have good intentions where you are concerned, but as I said before, don't close your eyes to anyone. Well-meaning people will change. You can trust them, but trust them also to be human. Humans sometimes fail. When you know a person is capable of disappointing you, you should not trust them with your life. God is the only one that you should trust with your life. I've learned never to say what I would not do, but pray that God will keep me from doing anything that is not pleasing to Him or is detrimental to my fellow man. I think this is at best what you can expect from any human being. To ask for anything else would be asking for more than God has ever gotten out of man.

I've heard people say I would not do this, that, or the other, but under what circumstances has it been said? A well-nourished man on any given day will say he would not eat out of the garbage or drink from polluted water, but if he is starving to death, you may get a different answer. You cannot trust your girlfriend to be infallible, but you can trust her to have good intentions. A person who has good intentions and somehow falls into a moment of weakness can be better understood when they ask for your forgiveness. On the other hand, if a person betrays you and never confesses even when the truth comes to light, you will know that this person is not to be trusted. To trust is to believe for the best, but understanding is to forgive when trust has been breached.

We Understand Each Other

The Bible declares that wisdom is the principle lesson to be learned in this life; second only to wisdom is a good understanding. To understand is to pardon. I may not agree with a person who sells their body for a living, but if they grew up in this type of environment, or possibly have been molested over the years, I could understand why they do what they do. I may not agree with a person who steals for a living, but if this was the last resort to feeding a starving body, I would understand. I may not agree with a person who practices homosexuality, but I understand that this lifestyle is a choice and if this is their choice, I will respect them for who they are. People who understand each other can better build lasting relationships than those who don't. When you see people who have established strong bonds among themselves, it is usually because they choose to understand and forgive one another. You will never agree all the time with any one person, not even yourself. In order for you to build a strong bond, you must have had the relationship tested over time. It is the moment of truth after the test that determines the life of the relationship. Once again, to understand is to pardon.

Women for the longest time have been building stronger bonds than men, because they live from a totally different perspective than men. This may sound funny, but I know it to be the truth. Sometimes women will band together just to oppose men. This is not a good thing to do, but it happens. Women bond on a number of issues. No one but another woman can relate to the subject of carrying a baby. Women understand each other when men lie about their involvement with other females. Women understand that men see them as weak, but they know who it is that holds the bond together in the family. This is a unique gift that God has given to women, and this is why you are more able to move on when things don't turn out well rather than hanging out on the streets drowning your sorrows with a beer. Women as well as men are drinking alcohol and smoking dope, but the ratio is much higher in men when it comes to addiction. A woman can manage a house with four or five children when the average men cannot manage it with one. You understand each other as girlfriends and as women, because your hearts are a little closer to God than the average man. This is why women overwhelmingly support the church more than men. Women as a whole are looking for love and will sometimes go to drastic measures to get it. But men want power, and we will go to any length to get it. If the understanding that many women have was in the heart of men, the world would be a safer place to live.

I'm Out With the Girls

Every man needs to give his woman freedom to spend some time with her girlfriends. While I do believe that your husband or your fiancée should be your best friend, they should not be your only friend. When you understand the dynamics of what I talked about in the previous segment, you will know that there are certain things that can only come from another woman as it relates your life. This time alone that women share helps to foster the ties that hold our communities together. I encourage women to get together, because it helps me in my endeavors. I know that I can sometimes be stoic, so if I can sometimes pawn my wife off on someone who is not out to undermine our relationship, it makes me happy. Of course, as I said earlier, I don't want her giving more time to other people than I get, but I want to share her with others.

I really do admire how women can get together and talk for hours and never seem to get bored. Men, on the other hand, can normally tolerate about ten minutes unless it's about a business deal or sports. My wife and her mother are on the phone three to five times a day, talking about the same things they talked about the day before. If they don't have anything to talk about, they will make up something. When I talk to my dad, it is usually about a project or occasionally we will talk about church business. Women know how to find common ground and keep a bond going and we need this to take place in our world.

I want you women to continue building bonds and showing men that you do not need to have a reason to get together other than just to share one another's thoughts. Guys have always known the power of female bonding and this is why many of them are jealous of your relationships. Men are more selfish with their time while women are more generous. I remember growing up watching my mother and her sisters-in-law going to one another's houses from time to time, just to talk to one another. Even today, my sisters talk to each far more than the guys. I am of the opinion that the greatest blessings in life are those relationships that last throughout a lifetime. Striving after position, money, and power is the most frustrating things a man can do. Perhaps this is why women overall live longer and healthier lives than men.

The list of benefits of female bonding can go on and on because so much of the freedom that we enjoy as men is the result of women being who they are. I'm not mad at you; keep the relationships strong and God is going to reward you for the unselfish service that you give to the kingdom of God and to the world. Ladies, you have my support when it comes to your time with each other. I understand the value of it and I hope that our men will catch on. I don't want to see another generation pass without bridging the gap in our community.

Entertainment: Where to Draw the Line

In Ecclesiastes 3, King Solomon says that there is a time for everything. I suppose this includes entertainment. The Bible declares in the Book of Proverbs that a merry heart does good like medicine. Entertainment is designed specifically to bring pleasure. There has been a mind-set in the church for years which suggests that entertainment is not for saints. I told you in on the previous chapters that I grew up in a very traditional family and church. Sports of any sort, movies, even swimming were looked upon as being unspiritual. People who did such things were considered carnal. As I grew older and more mature in the faith, I began to scrutinize these teachings and discovered that the activity was not wrong, but the way in which we engage in them could be. In essence, you must know where to draw the line when it comes to these things and any other areas in this world if you intend to stay focused on your purpose here on Earth.

The apostle Paul admonished Timothy in 2 Timothy 3:1–4, "This know also, that in the last days perilous times shall come. For men shall be lovers of their own selves, covetous, boasters, proud, blasphemers, disobedient to parents, unthankful, unholy, Without natural affection, trucebreakers, false accusers, incontinent, fierce, despisers of those that are good, Traitors, heady, highminded, lovers of pleasures more than lovers of God." The key words of this verse are, "lovers of pleasures more than lovers of God." What I gather from this passage is that people who desire to have pleasure more than God are in the wrong.

I do believe that there are wholesome, balanced, cultural activities that godly women can do as favorite pasttimes. I don't believe that we should hang out in nightclubs listening to vulgar music or comedy to be entertained. I don't think that we should become running buddies with people who do. You are ambassadors of the kingdom of God and as His representative. You must be careful because the message you send could lead someone else astray. I can only think of one good reason for a saint to go in a club and that would be for the purpose of sharing the gospel. As far as the movies, much of what is produced crosses the line of clean entertainment, but there are some shows that are wholesome and carry a decent message about everyday life that I see no wrong in watching. As a child of God and a woman of Zion, your commitment does not end when you leave church. Entertainment can cover a wide range of things and clean fun is a gift from God. The Bible declares in Proverbs 17:22, "A merry heart doeth good like a medicine: but a broken spirit drieth the bones."

The Superior Woman's Challenge for Chapter 6

1. Having friends is the sign of a fulfilled, happy woman, but too many friends is the sign of a busy women. Which of the two do you want to be?

2. If you have a friend who has a lot of issues with men, she may destroy your relationship or hinder you from ever getting one. Avoid women who are so hardened by past or present issues that they refuse to let go. If you can, help them to get free of the problems that are causing their pain.

3. A girlfriend should be one you can trust at all times. If you are not sure about the trust, don't call her a girlfriend but an associate.

4. To trust people does not mean to give them carte blanche over every area of your life. Only God deserves this; however, you should feel comfortable in knowing that your friends have your best interest at heart.

5. Women have a special gift from God to foster strong bonds and relationships. Use this gift to build your community and not a clique that will cause division among your sisters.

6. Join a women's group or begin to build one in your church or organization. It will serve as a major stabilizing force within your ranks.

7. When you go out with the girls, make sure that your husbands are not the center of the conversation, unless it is a mutual support group to build better relationships at home.

8. If you are married no one should be your best friend but your husband.

Journal

Use this section to log special events (i.e., spiritual breakthroughs, special messages, meeting of new friends, etc.).

Week 1

_____

_____

_____

_____

_____

_____

Week 2

_____

_____

_____

_____

_____

_____

Week 3

Week 4

And Deborah, a prophetess, the wife of Lapidoth, she judged Israel at that time.

—Judges 4:4

Chapter 7

BUILDING HER COMMUNITY

If it takes a village to raise a child, then women are the keepers of the village, and it is the bonding of women that makes the community habitable.

WITH THE EXCEPTION OF politics and the military, women are at the front of basically every community activity. Based on the mere fact that women have a propensity to build strong bonds between themselves, their participation in community activities is extremely important. When we look at what goes on in neighborhood associations, sporting activities with children, voting, shopping in the malls and supermarkets, the movies, church activities, etc., you are up front. I cannot tell you the last time I went to the school to check on my children's classroom activities, but my wife is in the trenches getting the details every week. Of course, I keep abreast by means of her giving me the details of what is going on. It is not that I do not care, because it is very important to me that my children are active in their academics, but she is more driven than I am in this area. Our communities have weakened a great deal over the years as a result of misplaced values. I am convinced that when we had fewer things to distract us, our concentration on one another was different. With the increase of electronic gadgets such as computers and telephones, and more access to automobiles, we have become a lot more independent over the past thirty years.

The church is by far the strongest remaining entity in our communities throughout the Unites States and across the world. Women are the majority in most of the congregations and without you, most of our churches would be depleted in much of these active areas. With this kind of influence and presence by women throughout our society, it is incumbent upon you to evaluate the kind of relationships that you are building. I continue to talk about the decline over the years of moral and spiritual values in our communities, and women must also take their share of the blame. Statistics have proven that drug use, sexual promiscuity, and violence among women is on the rise.

Despite this, I happen to believe that the restoration of kingdom values is coming back to our communities and women will once again be the forerunners at making it happen. The increasing numbers of illegitimate children, the corrupting of men through irresponsible sex, as well as the fighting of young women over men is baffling. The vast majority of the bickering that goes on between young girls has to do with young boys. This is a sickness and disease of the mind that has crippled many of our young men and women. Somewhere and somehow, we must recapture the spirit of community relationships again. We need women of prayer, virtue, and power to begin reaching out to build strong bonds across racial, religious, and class lines. If we claim Christ as our Lord, we must model His life. He was a reformer, community activist, and lover of all people. When we see the world through His eyes, it will cause us to break the barrier of bondage and seek freedom for all humanity.

Supporting the PTA

Learning begins at home, and when a child leaves the home, nearly one-third of the day is spent in public school. One of the greatest needs is to have active women following through with their children in the schools. Statistics have proven that children whose parents are actively involved in their lives perform better in school. With the breakdown in our communities, especially in the public schools, you cannot afford to pawn your children off on a stranger for eight hours a day and not know what is going on in their lives. Women have always played a strong role in their children's education, but there are too many women today that have left their posts. Many of them are overly involved in social and church programs when our children are being neglected. I am not telling you not to be involved in church, but too much of what we call *church* is not church at all. It is futile to spend countless hours in church every week while your children are falling through the cracks for the lack of involved parents. Before there was ever a church building, church was in the home. We make such a big deal about prayer being out of the public schools, but we don't pray with our children at home.

I don't want you to think that I am putting a guilt trip on you as women, but you are usually the ones who are there for your children. We already know that many of our men are not actively involved in their children's lives, so you cannot drop the ball. I encourage you to purchase a copy of God's Man: *Prophet, Priest, and King* in the Destiny 2000 and Beyond Family Series. This book will transform your man's life if he applies the principles. As of now, God is expecting you to put in quality time in your community. I talk a lot about churches making the connection in our communities because the church is the strongest entity that we have. I want to encourage you to become a committee of one to develop some strategies to build your community. The Parent Teacher Association is only one way for you to get involved in making a difference.

One of the most frustrating places to be in life is a state of ignorance about what you have been called to do by God. If you begin to seek God about what He has designed you to do in this life, He will direct you to the right places to find those answers. From this day forward, if you will begin looking for a way to make a positive impact in your community, even if you do not have children or children in school, there is a place for you. There are thousands of women who are living unfulfilled lives because they have not found their niche. If you really want to make a difference in this life, start from this very moment by doing what Jacob did in Genesis 32:26. He wrestled all night with the angel of God until he got what he needed. You can do the same thing if you want to be blessed and used by God.

Community Activism and Politics

Politics has been a thorn in the side of many believers because we have been taught to believe that the two do not mix. One interpretation of the Constitution demands the separation faith and politics has crippled the church in many ways. For the past forty years, we have allowed the secular community to all but hijack the government of the Unites States. It is absolutely insane to suggest that politics and religion do not mix in this country, and at the same time, say that the country was founded on biblical principles. That would be like trying to take the air out of oxygen. If people who go to church every Sunday claim to worship God, how can the same people institute a government and exclude God. If God is in you when you go to church, He cannot be out of you when you go to work or pass laws to live by. This can be true under one circumstance—you would have to be a hypocrite. *Hypocrite* in the original Greek means "playactor." Perhaps this is all that God means to many Americans.

I want to challenge you as a believer in Christ to rethink this whole issue if you are one of the ones caught in this dilemma. We have been backpeddling for the past thirty years, tearing down something that it has taken nearly four hundred years to build. We all know at this point in the history of America that something was fundamentally wrong with the practices of many of the founding fathers of the nation, but the foundation they laid was right. When African-Americans and many whites were marching for the equal rights of blacks, not one element of the Constitution had to be changed, but simply enforced.

It is absolutely impossible for any citizen not to be affected by the political process because *politics* by definition means making and enforcing laws that apply to citizens. In essence, you cannot escape being involved because it is all about you. You can choose not to exercise your God-given right, but that will not change your involvement. If I had ten thousand dollars in a banking institution and the bank was earning interest off the investments of each of its customers, the bank would reap the benefit of my money even if I did not believe in earning interest. I am simply trying to tell you that there is no getting around the political aspect of life, so you might as well enjoy the benefits. Jesus made this statement in Matthew 9:37–38, "Then saith he unto his disciples, The harvest truly is plenteous, but the labourers are few; Pray ye therefore the Lord of the harvest, that he will send forth labourers into his harvest." You are His laborers, called to His harvest in order to reap an eternal blessing. The time will come when you will be rewarded for your service here on Earth, and your reward will be commensurate with the service you gave.

The Superior Woman's Challenge for Chapter 7

1. An ancient African proverb says, "It takes a village to raise a child." The spirit of independence has crippled our community; commit to become more involved in community activities that will empower your community with strong spiritual values.

2. If Jesus were here today, He would have the same agenda He had two thousand years ago: healing the sick, empowering the weak, and speaking out against corruption, beginning with those who make and execute the laws. His disciples did the same thing. Are you one of His children? If so, you should be doing the same thing.

3. Spiritual community activism is nothing more than promoting the kingdom of God on Earth; every believer has been assigned to do it.

4. Study the life and works of Jesus in the four Gospels and begin to pattern your lifestyle after Him.

5. If you have children in school, support your local PTA and encourage other mothers to do the same. If need be, offer someone a ride to the meeting.

6. Regardless of what you think of the political process, it is one in which to make your voice heard; take advantage of the process and trust God to honor your effort.

7. Taking an active role in politics can be frustrating, but if you believe God has called you to this area as a profession, don't hesitate to prepare yourself to get involved. He will give you the grace to be successful in all that you do.

8. Neither Republicans nor Democrats represent spirituality, but you can.

Journal

Use this section to log special events (i.e., spiritual breakthroughs, special messages, meeting of new friends, etc.).

Week 1

Week 2

Week 3

Week 4

Go, gather together all the Jews that are present in Shushan, and fast ye for me, and neither eat nor drink three days, night or day: I also and my maidens will fast likewise; and so will I go in unto the king, which is not according to the law: and if I perish, I perish.

—Esther 4:16

Chapter 8

WE ARE LEADERS, TOO

Leadership is influence. Women lead from behind the scenes every day, so why can't they lead in the forefront?

I said this before and I think it is worth repeating, I believe that a woman can do anything a man can do in ministry. However, I do not believe a woman should aspire to do everything a man does. When it comes to leading, women throughout history have proven to be ready, willing, and able to do the job. In this chapter, I will highlight a few women from biblical history who left a proven record of good leadership. John Maxwell says that leadership is nothing more than influence. After reading this sentence in his book, I decided to look up the word *influence* and here is what I found: The word *influence* means to pour in fluid. I simply used my common sense and figured out the rest. To pour in fluid means to have something invested within a vessel. If a person has influence in your life, it means that they have poured something into you. I suppose this is the reason why music and hip-hop culture have had such an impact in the lives of so many of our young people. They have poured in the fluid of music and entertainment into the lives of our youth, and this is why there is such an allegiance to the culture. I hope you get the point exactly the way it came home to me.

Women have poured into men and other women in so many ways, and their ability to lead is solely based on this fact. Some women have more influence in the lives of men and women than other men will ever have. Many women bring compassion to leadership that is lacking in a lot of men. Even if a woman is not the immediate leader in many cases, people are still looking for her presence to bring balance and credibility to the leadership. I know for a fact that my wife in many ways helps my leadership because she has such a nonthreatening personality. I have been told by many people who did not know me that they had initially formed the wrong opinion of me. I do understand how this happens even though it is not deliberate on my part. I am usually in such a serious state of mind that I don't notice my expressions most of the time. I readily smile when I talk one-on-one, but if I'm just sitting or reading, I have a serious look about me.

God has endowed women with the ability to communicate, build relationships, and make friends much faster than men. We are more skeptical and analytical in our approach towards each other. While statistics still prove that women and men choose male leadership over female, I believe that this has much to do with cultural conditioning, not any inferiority in women. When we speak of leadership, our subject should be the person with the most knowledge and ability to get the job done as opposed to the gender of the individual. You have my vote of confidence in your ability to lead; stay humble and God will use you mightily. Deborah went down in history as the only female judge in the Bible. She lived during a period when there was no king in Israel. The role of a judge was to mitigate civil issues and keep the people informed of their commitment to God. They were also known to be fierce warriors who were able to rally the nation to war in order to protect themselves from foreign enemies.

Deborah was not just a judge; she was also a prophetess. A prophetess was one who forth tells or foretells of God's curse or favor for the nation. According to Judges 4:5, Deborah judged the nation from under a palm tree which was called the "palm tree of Deborah." Deborah became known for her strategic implementation of a plan to bring victory to the nation. She summoned Barak to put his forces on the ground to fight against Sisera who was the commander of the army of Jabin, king of Canaan, who had terrorized Israel for twenty years. Barak was told by Deborah to prepare the forces and go to war on behalf of the nation and he would get victory. Barak's response was, I will go but only if you accompany me in the battle. Deborah and Barak's army numbered only ten thousand, while Sisera had a stronger army with many more fighters and nine hundred chariots of iron. When Barak decided that he would only go if Deborah went alongside him, she told Barak she would go, but that he would not get credit for winning the battle. She said to him that God would give the credit to a woman. As a result of Deborah's skillful planning, Israel defeated Sisera's army and all of his men were killed in battle. He was the only one that did not get killed on the battlefield but through the cunning act of a female, he died as a result of a peg driven through his head.

One of the admirable things about Deborah was that she was not trying to take any credit for this battle. She gave Barak the battle plan that was sure to bring victory but he decided that Deborah had to go along with him. I owned a radio station once and my office manager, who was a woman, had a sign pasted up in the office that had these words written on it: "Do you want to see the man in charge, or the woman who knows what is going on around here?" This is just one of the classic stories of the good leadership abilities that women possess. Women become leaders for the same reasons that men become leaders. It boils down to how much you know about the matter at hand, and how much fortitude, character, and stamina you have to get the job done. If God called you and placed within you certain leadership abilities, you do not have to compromise your ability to appease a man who is not willing to do the job. Just simply follow the leading of God and get the victory for the kingdom of God. However, you must remember that the victory is God's, and the glory belongs to Him alone.

Esther

The story of Esther is probably one of the most dramatic narratives in the Bible. You might consider it to be the story of true character and inner beauty which never lost its focus. Great power almost always ends up corrupting the individual in one way or another. Esther, however, has proven that you can be beautiful, powerful, and influential, yet still remain spiritual and humble. She led her people through one of the greatest struggles of their history during their period of exile in Babylon and Persia. She will always be remembered for this famous statement: "…and if I perish, I perish." I encourage you to read her entire legacy in the Book of Esther. You will learn about her triumphant rise to power from being an orphan to a queen.

Esther, whose name means "star," was chosen to become the wife of Xerxes, King of Persia, during the restoration period of the Jews. King Ahasuerus, or Xerxes, which he was also known as, became irate when his wife Vashti refused his request to parade her beauty before the officials of Persia. He had drunk himself into a drunken stupor and was obviously up to no good. Theologians suggest that he wanted his wife to parade naked and disgrace her honor before all at the king's palace. When she refused his request, the officials of Persia told the king that her rebellion would cause their wives to treat them in the same manner if he did not reprimand her. In his anger, he dismissed Vashti as his wife and began to audition the young virgins of Susa to take her place. Esther was one of those virgins that paraded before the king and he was taken by her beauty. Consequently, she became the next queen of Persia.

Esther's courageous leadership ability surfaced when wicked Haman, the king's assistant, deceitfully plotted to destroy the Jews. Haman, enraged because he could not get Esther's uncle, Mordecai, to bow before him, attempted to commit genocide on all Jews in the province of Susa. Mordecai reminded Esther, who had become queen, not to forget her true heritage, even though she had become queen of the empire. Esther told the king of the plot and Haman lost his position and his life as a result of his evil scheme. She vowed to go to the king even though she was not summoned to do so. Approaching the king without the proper protocol could have cost Esther her life. This single act of heroism put her uncle Mordecai as second-in-command of the kingdom and won the Jews, her own people, the freedom to exercise their culture in Persia without fear of reprisal from those who hated their cause. Her leadership, not her gender, was what made her great.

New Testament Women Leading the Way

Elizabeth, the mother of John the Baptist, and Mary, the mother of Jesus, were the first two women who gained prominence in the New Testament. Both of these women played a leading role in ushering in the Messiah and both had a strong presence in their community. Elizabeth was the wife of a priest, who was named Zacharias. The position of first lady carried the same amount of clout and stress as it does today. Anytime you are married to the leader, whether you are up front or in the background, you are also carrying the load of leadership. Women who are married to leaders will always bear their share of the load simply because husbands usually put their load on them. Even if he chooses not to share his burden with her, what he does not say will be just as burdening.

Jesus' mother Mary, Mary Magdalene, Mary the sister of Martha, and Martha are just a few of the women who played an active role in the ministry of Jesus. He confided in them in many ways, as well as enjoyed their companionship during His numerous appearances as He carried out His public ministry. It was the women who arrived first at the tomb of Jesus after His resurrection.

The apostle Paul embraced numerous women during his course of ministry. He acknowledged the mother of Timothy, Eunice, and Grandmother Lois as being great women of faith. They were responsible for putting in the great foundation that prepared Him for the ministry. As you read throughout the remainder of Paul's ministry, other women were associated with him. Even though he admonished those women who stepped over the boundaries as it related to their roles within the culture, he spared no pain in giving credit to the women who were leaders in their own right. From the Old Testament, into the New Testament and all through medieval and modern history, women have made their mark in the hall of faith. You too can join the rank of leadership if you are willing to meet the challenge that it takes to do the job.

I believe that God is assigning roles to women in a strategic manner in order to birth the kingdom of God in this last hour. It is time for men and women to understand that God does not have a hang-up with female leadership. It is the male leadership that is missing; that is what He has the problem with. If more men would take their places on the front line, they would gladly welcome all the help they could get to fight the power of darkness. When we fully learn that the kingdom of God is not about flesh and blood, but about love, peace, and joy in the Holy Spirit, we can begin to use that united force to destroy the works of darkness and bring glory to God. If you know your place, stay the course; if you don't, God will direct you if you seek Him.

The Superior Woman's Challenge for Chapter 8

1. You may not be a pastor, but you are a leader in the kingdom of God. Develop your leadership skills by studying under mentors and teachers who are trained in the area you feel led to work in.

2. Become familiar with all of the leading women in the Bible and model their leadership skills in your life.

3. If you are working in an area that is dominated by men, be very discrete in your behavior towards them. Should you become a target of sexual harassment, begin to think of ways to avoid this type of situation. Do not let your good be spoken of in a negative way.

4. A man's stereotypical attitude towards females in leadership can be real in their minds, however, do not overcompensate by trying to impress men. You are working for God, and this is all that matters.

5. As a leader, you are going to be judged by your ability to get the job done with the least amount of distraction and rejection from your subordinates, which is the same standard men are judged by. In essence, you must think and function as a leader, not as a woman.

6. People may not always like your leadership style, but they will respect you if you can prove that you know what you are doing.

7. As a leader, you do not need to know how to do everything yourself, but you do need to know how to get the job done.

8. To handle yourself, use your head; to handle others, use your heart.

Journal

Use this section to log special events (i.e., spiritual breakthroughs, special messages, meeting of new friends, etc.).

Week 1

_____
_____
_____
_____
_____
_____

Week 2

_____
_____
_____
_____
_____
_____

Week 3

Week 4

She seeketh wool, and flax, and worketh willingly with her hands. She is like the merchants' ships; she bringeth her food from afar. She riseth also while it is yet night, and giveth meat to her household, and a portion to her maidens. She considereth a field, and buyeth it: with the fruit of her hands she planteth a vineyard.

—Proverbs 31:13–16

Chapter 9

The Professional Woman

If a woman is functioning in the corporate arena, doing the same job as a man and getting the same pay, chances are she is more qualified than he is.

Women have proven time and time again that they are willing, capable, and qualified to do basically anything a man can do. You have broken the barriers of separation as professionals and have proven that you are equipped to carry your load in the professional arena. When the Bible speaks of the woman being the weaker vessel, it has nothing to do with her spiritual, emotional, or intellectual capabilities. Biologically, her physique in most cases is not as strong as a man's—but that has everything to do with the beauty of God's design. Having said this, I do believe there are some jobs that women should shy away from simply because of this reason.

Many women have gone out of their way to compete with men in some of the areas that call for brawns over brains, and these fields of pursuit have taken a great toll on their bodies. I'm not speaking as an authority when I make this statement; but I assume that some women pursue these areas because this is all that is left for them. I don't want to assume that they are doing it just to prove a point. Perhaps if more men were being responsible, our women could focus on things that are more compatible with their physical structure. I believe that women should always maintain their femininity. When I see females jumping off of garbage trucks, climbing light poles, or even holding up the front line in war, I take personal issue with it. Perhaps it's the way I was raised, because I never saw my mom so much as mow the lawn. My dad was into construction work as long as I can remember, yet I have never seen my mom work on a construction site. I'm not saying that it hasn't happened over the sixty years of their marriage, but I haven't seen it. Maybe she went to hang out with him a time or two as he wrapped up a job, but not to work.

I would be the first to tell you that women should develop a financially profitable lifestyle for themselves. When a woman is raising children who need the nurturing that only a mother is designed to give, I think that much of her time should be spent in the home; beyond this, she should be totally free to pursue some type of fulfilling career outside of the home. This may sound a bit overwhelming at the moment of transition but it will prove to be rewarding if you put forth the effort. The fastest growing demographic of small business owners is female. God will give you the wisdom, direction, and energy to reach these goals. Of course, if she desires to live at home as a full-time housewife, this is her choice. I'm only trying to say that too many women stop living when the children are grown. You should be thinking of ways in which to further your purpose in the kingdom of God once the responsibilities of raising your little ones are done. Your responsibilities as a wife and a mother make up the primary roles that God has defined for women. The role as a wife will continue until death but raising children is only for a season.

You will be a mother for life but you should have taught and trained your children to go on and become parents on their own who will not need you to hold their hands all the way through life. A good mother will give her children wings to fly so they can live a complete life apart from the parents. This by no means suggests that you will entirely cut ties with them, but they need to know how to fend for themselves. Some parents cripple their children's futures by keeping them dependent for life. Many children don't have a life because they have to use all their means to support the parents. Of course, if the parents are ill and not able to do for themselves, this is the role of the children. In many places throughout the world, there are no social security benefits to fall back on. In the late eighties I had an occasion to take a vacation to Seoul, South Korea, and I remember vividly I was told that there was no welfare system in South Korea.

Becoming a professional is a noble thing to do in my opinion, as long as it does not compromise the family structure. Since women are generally the ones that spend most of the time with the children during their formative years, their absence could possibly impair the children in some way. Of course, I know there are exceptions to every rule, but you probably agree that children are generally closer to their mother early on in life. The moral and spiritual degeneration in our society can be traced back to two things—the absence of sound moral principles and the breakdown of the family. In fact, when you talk about moral values, all we know on this subject comes directly or indirectly from the Bible. It still baffles me to see how our leaders in government and some in the church ignore the biblical values that were responsible for making America what it is.

When you study the history of the Roman Empire, you learn that this thriving nation came to a screeching halt as moral and spiritual values were neglected. Throughout history, especial with the nation of Israel, these principles hold true. God knew exactly what He was doing when He designed the family structure. The devil also knew and this is why he has done everything possible to destroy the foundation of society, the family.

As women, you have always played a pivotal role in keeping the community strong, even though you weren't given credit for doing so. No amount of money can take the place of strong spiritual and family values. It would be better for you to live on a salary of thirty thousand dollars per year with your family intact, than a one hundred thousand dollar salary with your family torn apart. Too many of us are driven to get more things rather than more of God. Pursue your professional career but not at the expense of losing your family or becoming too busy to start one.

Schoolteachers

Women also make up the majority of teachers in our public schools. My speculation as to why this is true has everything to do with the compassion and willingness of women to pass on the nurturing spirit that God has placed within them. After all, it is the mothers who overwhelmingly invest in children at an early age, teaching them much of what will cling to them for a lifetime. The desire in women to teach children is the very essence of motherhood. Men for the most part do not possess the tolerance, patience, or commitment to teach children in a traditional classroom. This is why there are so few male teachers. Men have a more hands-on teaching style, and I believe the public schools have failed our students and our men is this area. I talked about this area in my book, *Rite of Passage,* so I will not spend much time on the subject here since this book is for women. I encourage you to maintain this passion that is burning within you to teach, even though it may get tough sometimes. The breakdown in our society in the areas of the family does not help the cause of teachers at all. If a child does not have the proper foundation in the home, it puts a tremendous amount of strain on the teachers in the classroom.

The breakdown that exists all over our society is the reason why the Destiny 2000 and Beyond Family Series was birthed. I would like to take this time to encourage you as a schoolteacher to begin standing up for spiritual values and help to return these principles to our schools. There is an all-out conspiracy to overthrow the biblical foundation that has existed in this country from its inception. While I do not agree with many of the practices that were brought over in the birthing of America, I believe the forefathers put the right thing in place as the foundation—the Bible. In fact, if you study the history of the school system in our country, you will find that the church was responsible for putting it in place. Some of the greatest colleges and learning institutions in this country still embrace many of the biblical principles that we embrace in churches every Sunday.

If you are a schoolteacher, have been in the past, or are aspiring to become one, let me tell you that this is a noble profession. As a man, I have to say that having experienced it firsthand, boys will probably never have the respect for young female teachers that they have for men. This is not a blanket statement, but it is true for the most part. Young boys, depending on their ages, look at their young female teachers as sex symbols. This is normal behavior among boys when they are in the presence of females. Don't allow this to distract you from your duties; continue to teach by precepts and godly example.

Doctors

Female doctors, nurses, paramedics, EMTs, and the like have made tremendous strides in the medical field over the past fifty years. During the sexual revolution when women discovered that they could do more than just keep house, many of them headed for professional careers. Some of the best professionals in all areas in the medical field are women. You command a level of respect in the professional arena because you usually have to work harder than men to get the same credit. The struggle that exists among women is tantamount to that of African-Americans when it comes to being treated fairly in the professional field. To this day statistics have proven that there are women who do the very same job as men but for a lesser salary. Due to tougher discrimination laws, this practice in subtle, but sometimes it is uncovered and dealt with properly. Your participation in the professional field brings a sense of compassion that has served to balance out this area of our society. The fields traditionally dominated by men, especially white men, now have to reckon with the presence of bright, confident females who know what they are doing.

The competence that females bring to the workplace has raised the quality of health care overall. I think that for the same reasons females have the propensity to build stronger bonds than men, your professionalism also reaches a new level. I do want to say one thing that may seem a bit abrasive, but take it for love. As women, you should not ever allow your desire to be good in the workplace cause you to become competitive, callous, cold, or hard like many of your male coworkers. If this happens, you will be no different than the men you work alongside. One of the biggest fears that I've heard voiced among men is that the professional woman does not have boundaries. She wants to dominate men in every area. While I do know that there are many passive men who prefer to have the female in control of things, most men still want to feel like they are the authority when it comes to the home.

I want to encourage you once again to read the marriage book in the Destiny 2000 and Beyond Family Series in order to achieve clarity regarding the roles God gave to men versus women. If being the professional is going to lessen your effectiveness as a loving and kind lady, you may want to reconsider your quest for professionalism. I hope that the insight I'm sharing is coming across the way it is intended, because the last thing I want to do is get on the bad side of females. However, I do believe that you want to know what men are thinking, and since I am one, I believe I speak for many men. Continue to give to the medical profession the touch that only a woman can give.

Lawyers

Women account for a large percentage of the attorneys in the world. We need only to read the Book of Judges to see that this is an area where females are also very competent. In the wake of reality television, female judges are topping the charts in the ratings. When dealing with the law, it simply takes someone with the brilliance to interpret the letter of the law. As opposed to the letter of the law, there is such a thing as common sense, and much of it has gone completely out the window. I want to personally thank God for women who know the letter of the law, and along with the letter, how to apply common sense. I have said it before and I will say it again—I think that a woman can do anything a man can do, and when it comes to being a good lawyer, women are some of the best. Once again, the professionalism is not compromised in any way by the fact that a woman is doing the job. I am looking for the day when a woman will join the Supreme Court justices in helping to get

America back on track. Once again, I must keep referring to the side of females that I know is stronger than men and that is the ability to be compassionate. It is this strength that women bring to every area of the professional field. If women stay focused and always remain true to their hearts, they will not let the power and position they hold keep them from making sound judgments when it comes to the law.

I have seen some women who try so hard to compete or exceed men that they simply become an embarrassment to women themselves. This is why I believe some women still overwhelmingly vote for men in politics. As a lawyer, always remember that God is the ultimate Lawgiver and you are representing him when you adjudicate concerning the lives of humanity. Continue to represent God and women in what you do.

Bankers

You will find female professionals in every walk of life. The banking industry has its share of women bankers as well as female millionaires. Women are a force in our society that will not be ignored at any level. When it comes to managing money, I personally believe that women do a better job than men. Women generally mature faster than men and this maturity includes handling money. As I am writing this book, I'm preparing to go to a seminar that will be given by a woman on how to handle finances. The banking industry, especially the bank tellers, is flooded with women. In fact, if I go to a bank that has a man working the counter or the drive through, I think of him as being out of place. It is just a natural instinct simply because these jobs have been dominated by women for so long. I do know that does not necessarily make him a softy, but it's just the way things have become. I feel the same way about schoolteachers; when I see a male teacher, it is almost strange. Since women are constantly moving to the forefront in business, it would make sense for them to manage much of the industry.

Listed below are some statistics taken from www.us-banker.com concerning the progress that women are making in the banking industry. "Women in banking are indeed an awesome force. They are gaining more seats as board directors, comprising 13.4 percent of those at commercial banks in 2003, up from 10 percent in 2001; 14.1 percent of those at diversified financial firms, up from 9 percent; and 11.3 percent at securities' firms, up from 8 percent, according to research by Catalyst. The percentage of female corporate officers in commercial banks rose to 15.2 percent in 2002, up from 11.8 percent in 2000; represented 23.6 percent of those in diversified financial firms, up from 20.2 percent; but slid to 10.6 percent in the securities industry, down from 11.3 percent."

The strides that women are making in basically every area of our society has much to do with men coming to terms with the intelligence of women. Racism, bigotry, and sexism afforded men in this country, particularly white men, an advantage in the past that is swiftly eroding. As you continue to pursue God's direction for your life, He will direct you in the key areas of your career that will better serve His kingdom here on Earth.

CEOs

A CEO is the Chief Executive Officer of a corporation, or independent business, and the numbers of female CEOs are growing as well. As the CEO, you generally get the opportunity to make the final decision on both important and trivial issues. This can sometimes be overwhelming, but women once again have proven that they have what it takes to do the job. Here is a quote that comes directly from an article written by John Getting and David Johnson during Woman's History Month in 2005: "But although women make up half of America's labor force, still only two Fortune 500 companies have women CEOs or presidents, and 90 of those 500 companies don't have any women corporate officers. Catalyst, the not-for-profit New York-based women's research organization, points out, however, that its data shows a change over the last five years. A recent survey revealed that 10% of the Fortune 500 companies have women holding at least one-quarter of their corporate officer positions. This percentage rose from only 5% in 1995." (Quote found at infoplease.com/spot/womenceo1.html.)

I stated before that women have been held back for a long time—due in part to a male-dominated workforce, and in part to their own volition, which stems from their commitment to the home. As demanding as the job of a CEO is, some of these women have managed to maintain their roles as a mother and wife as well. I must admit, when I compare what I do on an average day to what my wife does, sometimes I really feel I'm coming up short. I do not have the tolerance or the skills to manage the children the way she does. I can very well make them behave but I admire her skills to interact with them and keep them entertained all the time. I can see how women are able to do a good job in the workplace and come home and do a good job there also. Running a house is nothing less than running a corporation; it requires the ability to juggle several things at the same time, something that women have been doing for quite some time.

I am not sure how this statement will be taken by my fellow brothers, but I have been of the mind-set for some time that most women are quicker thinkers than men. I believe that the female instinct due to maternal makeup gives them an advantage in many ways. This is why I believe it is so important for both men and women to understand their roles in a relationship. Sometimes you may know more about an issue, but to have peace, you may have to allow your husband to find out certain things for himself. This principle can also hold true in the position as a CEO. You may be the one in charge, but to get people to work along with you, you will occasionally have to let them think they are having their way. Here is a secret: to handle yourself use your head, to handle others, use your heart. Continue to do well at what you do and use all of your recourses to enhance the kingdom of God here on Earth.

Prosperity: Whose It Is, What It Is, and Why It Is

The term *prosperity* is so prevalent among churches that it would be remiss of me if I did not address the topic. Prosperity by definition has to do with financial wealth. You can put a spin on it and include health, spirituality, and whatever else you choose. I specifically want to deal with the wealth aspect of it and try to give you some balance on the topic. Over the past twenty years or so, the term prosperity has been badly abused by gainsaying preachers, especially the so-called Word of Faith teachings. As I see it in Scripture, God has made it clear that He takes pleasure in the prosperity of servants. However, nowhere in Scripture does it say to seek God for prosperity of riches. On the contrary, He says that if we live right, prosperity will find us (Deuteronomy 28:2). When I listen to the teachings of prosperity so loosely handled by so many preachers, I begin to quiver, and wonder what Bible they are getting this message from. When I hear preachers challenging people to give a faith offering and trust God to get rich, I say to myself, *This is a gross misrepresentation of Scripture.* Jesus said in Matthew 6 that the Gentiles seek Him for things, or prosperity, but the children of the kingdom should seek the kingdom of God and its righteousness, and if they do, the things that are needed for this life will be added to them. The Gentiles were unbelievers or nations other than Israel.

Does God want His children to live in lack and poverty? No! But does He want His children to seek Him for riches or material things? No! He already knows that you need these things. Whenever God blesses anyone with riches, it is given for the benefit of His body, and not for one person or organization to flaunt things as a sign of God's blessings. He makes the sun to shine on the just as well as the unjust. To be rich is no more a sign of you being blessed by God than to weigh six hundred pounds is a sign of being healthy. What He wants from the people who are called by His name is to learn how to get along here on Earth. He is tired of the factions, cliques, and gangs that His body is divided into. He wants us to know that He died for His body, not severed body parts. He wants us to know that our strength is in one another and not in our arrogance and pride regarding what we have. The riches belong to Him. What He wants is for His body to become one as He and the Father are one, according to St. John 17:20–21. What He wants is for ministries and churches to stop the fighting and competitiveness that exist among them and come together for the good of the kingdom. He wants the body to take back the drug-infested, crime-ridden, and sexually-perverted areas of our cities, starting with the church, for the benefit of the kingdom.

God's Way to Financial Prosperity and Peace

God's way to financial prosperity and peace is what He desires for the children of His kingdom. No promise of prosperity from God should be taught without first teaching the principles of preparation. Teach people the need to go to school and learn a craft or skill. Take them to chapter one in this manual to learn how to prosper God's way. The preachers are taking the message of prosperity out of context. This is contaminating because it takes the focus off the gospel of transformation and puts it on the gospel of greed. If the preachers would tell you the truth, they would tell you that 95 percent of the money that is coming into the church is from poor and moderate income givers who work every day for their money. These are people who have burned the midnight oil to earn a decent education and have worked their way into a nice job and a career. You need to carefully read Deuteronomy 28 and Matthew 6 to learn what God is saying about you and your attitude toward material possessions. I recommend that you consult a financial advisor who can teach you the basic fundamentals of money management and investing if you desire to have financial solvency in your future. If you are deceived by the hype of gainsaying preachers, you will never have a future of peace and prosperity the way God desires for you. You may get a lot of things—but things will not give you peace. God wants you to have a clear understanding of what it means to be given the wealth of this world.

Every servant that He entrusts with abundant wealth is tried in the fire of persecution to ensure that he will know what to do with kingdom wealth. Abraham was blessed with riches, but one should read about his life before assuming that he easily gained them. Job was blessed with riches, but read about his life first. King Solomon was blessed with riches, but look at what happened to him at the end of his life. He inherited the wealth of the kingdom that his father David suffered for but he never learned beforehand how to handle wealth. Consequently, as he got older he totally forgot the God who allowed the wealth to be transferred into his hands. As a result of his lapse in judgment in his old age, he strayed away from God and died frustrated. He cursed the day he ever inherited the wealth. Ecclesiastes 6:1–2 says, "There is an evil which I have seen under the sun, and it is common among men: A man to whom God hath given riches, wealth, and honour, so that he wanteth nothing for his soul of all that he desireth, yet God giveth him not power to eat thereof, but a stranger eateth it: *this is vanity, and it is an evil disease*" (emphasis added).

The greatest need in the body of Christ is for us to learn how to live by kingdom principles. We have been treating each other in a worldly fashion. When kingdom prosperity comes to the body of Christ, we will know how to properly handle and distribute wealth.

> If you can find a truly good wife, she is worth more than precious gems! Her husband can trust her, and she will richly satisfy his needs. She will not hinder him but help him all her life. She finds wool and flax and busily spins it. She buys imported foods brought by ship from distant ports. She gets up before dawn to prepare breakfast for her household and plans the day's work for her servant girls. She goes out to inspect a field and buys it; with her own hands she plants a vineyard. She is energetic, a hard worker, and watches for bargains. She works far into the night! She sews for the poor and generously helps those in need. She has no fear of winter for her household, for she has made warm clothes for all of them. She also upholsters with finest tapestry; her own clothing is beautifully made—a purple gown of pure linen. Her husband is well known, for he sits in the council chamber with the other civic leaders. She makes belted linen garments to sell to the merchants. She is a woman of strength and dignity and has no fear of old age. When she speaks, her words are wise, and kindness is the rule for everything she says. She watches carefully all that goes on throughout her household and is never lazy. Her children stand and bless

her; so does her husband. He praises her with these words: "There are many fine women in the world, but you are the best of them all!" Charm can be deceptive and beauty doesn't last, but a woman who fears and reverences God shall be greatly praised. Praise her for the many fine things she does. These good deeds of hers shall bring her honor and recognition from people of importance.
—Proverbs 31:10–31, TLB

When you read this passage, it may sound a bit overwhelming and almost impossible to do, but you can find your niche somewhere in here. As a woman you were created for one primary reason—to complete men. Living in a world without women would be like lying on beach sand without any water; wanting to eat but having no appetite; living in a house but not a home…you get the picture. This is the reason why men will go to extremities and even take a woman's life when she threatens to leave, because they feel hopeless without her. This is by no means an attempt to justify their behavior, but when men do this, it is a cry of the heart and a plea for help. When a man takes a woman's life under such terms, he is simply saying, "I am hopeless without you, and if I cannot have you, nobody else will." This behavior is by no means a sign of strength; it is a sign of depravity, weakness, and hopelessness. The Proverbs 31 woman is what it's going to take to rebuild our world; she is conquering her world through love. Make it your priority to become the woman of God that you were created to be. You have everything within you that is necessary to get started; therefore press toward the mark of the high calling in Christ Jesus.

The Superior Woman's Challenge for Chapter 9

1. Always remember that you are a child of God and a saint first, and second a professional woman. Everything you do should reflect the kingdom of God in a positive light.

2. As a professional, you should take every opportunity to let your clients and your associates know about your relationship with God.

3. You should set the atmosphere in the areas in which you operate; never allow your worldly clients to desecrate your workplace. Morality should be your number one motive as a professional, not money.

4. If there is an association of Christian professionals in your community, try to participate in the organization so as to build a strong link between your profession and the community.

5. As a professional woman, begin to look for ways to mentor young people in your church or organization.

6. Having a professional career can be quite demanding; always look for ways to balance your professional, church, and family life so as to not let any area go unattended.

7. If you are a single woman, be sure to discuss your career plans with your prospective mate when the time is right. This should normally come before the relationship is at the engagement level.

8. Never use your career or your income as a means to negate the role of your husband in the home. He is the spiritual priest of the home in the hierarchy which God has set up; it is your duty to allow this order to function properly.

Journal

Use this section to log special events (i.e., spiritual breakthroughs, special messages, meeting of new friends, etc.)

Week 1

_____

_____

_____

_____

_____

Week 2

_____

_____

_____

_____

_____

Week 3

Week 4

Beloved, I wish above all things that thou mayest prosper and be in health, even as thy soul prospereth.

—3 John 1:2

Chapter 10

GUARDING YOUR HEALTH

On this earth, your physical health is as important to God as your spiritual health; miraculous healing is a gift, but maintaining your health is your responsibility.

Your body is the most complex machine, if I may use this term, ever designed, and you would expect people to do a better job maintaining it, but we don't. As a whole, we are more careful with our automobile than we are with our body. If you bought a car and it required premium fuel, you would not put regular gas in the car. Perhaps with the rising gas prices you may consider it, but I think you get the point. We are more health conscious as a nation than we were thirty years ago, but we are also carrying more excess weight around than thirty years ago.

It all leads back to the same thing—ruling your flesh, or discipline. We want to rule everyone and everything except our own flesh. I believe that God is expecting us to be good stewards of our body as well. People can know good and well that something they are eating is not compatible with their metabolism, but against the doctor's orders they say, "Well, you've got to die from something." Do you know what that really means? You are essentially saying, "I could potentially live until I'm eighty, but I will settle for fifty or sixty." Instead of practicing discipline, we settle for pleasure.

I have been lactose intolerant all of my life but did not know it until two years ago. I actually discovered it on my own when I stopped to buy a milk shake. Only after sucking the first strawful did I feel this sensation in my stomach. God spoke to me and said, "It is the milk shake causing the discomfort." When I got home there was an article that my wife brought home on the subject of being lactose intolerant. The very same symptoms that I suffered from all of my life were precisely described in the article. That was the last drop of ice cream, milk, or milkshake that I ever consumed; I vowed never to drink it again. Anything that causes me to feel the way milk does will not go into my body. I enjoyed milk, ice cream, milk shakes, and all sorts of dairy products. However, once dairy products got into my system, they would build up over time and cause gas in my intestine. About once per month I would get so sick it felt like I was about to die, literally. I would go to the bathroom and try to move my bowels; it would take twenty to forty minutes. Sometimes I could feel the gas coming up in my shoulders and my arms. All the time I just thought that it was normal for me to have those complications. Sometimes we know that the things we are doing are killing us, but we don't have the will to stop. When I started drinking alcohol as a teenager I would get so drunk and sick that I would vow never to drink again, but I kept on drinking. I did not want to be in a drunken stupor, but I did not want to stop. The choice is yours: you can live to eat or eat to live. Your body is God's temple; treat it as such and you are more likely to live longer and healthier.

Milk does not affect everyone the same way, but animal milk is not for human consumption. I am sure there are things that you are eating too much of that are affecting you, and you know it. Just muster up the discipline and get rid of the junk. Your body is the temple of the Lord, why would you deliberately harm it? You would not consider smoking a cigarette, but you will consume beef and pork without a thought and both of them can cause cancer. We all know that our ultimate destiny and lifespan is in God's hands, but I think that it is wise to eat as healthy as possible.

Back in 1982 I was given a book called *Back to Eden* and it revolutionized my eating habits. I stopped eating all types of meat, "cold turkey," for over a year. Later I drifted back to fish and chicken, but no types of beef or pork ever again. Before you say it, I already know that our food supply, even the fruits and vegetables, have potentially harmful chemicals, but I'd rather take my chances with those than to eat food that was never designed for my body.

I also discovered that water is an excellent laxative, and began to drink plenty of it—eight to ten glasses daily. We talked about the pills in step four and there are some that you can use as laxatives. But water is by far the safest and least expensive laxative you can buy. Water does not taste good to most people until they become very thirsty. At this point it is equivalent to running your car out of water—the engine gets extremely hot, and then you pour in a cold glass of water to cool it down. If you did this to an engine it would crack the block; try doing it to a glass and see what it does. Put a glass in the freezer until it is frozen; then put some steaming hot water in the glass and watch the reaction. Now can you imagine how it affects your body when you wait until you are completely thirsty to drink? You must learn how to drink water out of habit and not thirst. Your body has over thirty feet of intestine and that is how far your food must travel before you can relieve the waste. Water is more prevalent than any other natural resources and we use it less than any other. As a child of destiny, you cannot afford to cut your journey short because you aren't willing to become disciplined in maintaining good health habits.

I believe that it is prudent to retain a good doctor and make reasonable visits. As a professional, he has taken the time to learn all of the vital organs and their functions. I don't believe that doctors are gods but God has allowed them to acquire the skills to advise us in many cases. However, there are times when the doctor may have exhausted his abilities and will resort to speculations; you must use the wisdom God gave you to distinguish the difference.

I sometimes liken the human body to an automobile. I've seen classic cars that have been around since the twenties and thirties complete with all of their original parts and running like a kitten (quiet). There are other cars that are less than ten years old and have been totally trashed by the owner. Perhaps you can take a good guess as to what made the difference in the two automobiles. Tired of guessing? Well it's simply the maintenance. If you take care of your body, maintain the proper diet, rest, and relaxation, keep your mind free from corruption, bathe often, and brush your teeth often, it is a scientific fact that you will live longer. A child of destiny will not make lame excuses like, "Well, you've got to die from something." Your body belongs to the Lord and He has only made you the steward; take care of His temple.

Menstruation and Menopause

Menstruation, also commonly known as a female's "period," is the monthly discharging of blood, secretions, and tissue debris from the uterus that occurs in nonpregnant women beginning as early as ten years of age, and continuing until menopause. I would like to note that it is not uncommon for some women to have their period for several months during pregnancy.

The menstrual cycle is known to cause certain affects upon the body and emotions. Some of the symptoms are as follows: a) headaches, b) dizziness, c) fainting spells, d) nausea and vomiting, e) mood swings, f) hot and cold flashes, g) cramps, h) fatigue, and i) cravings for certain types of food. Some women have even been known to commit violent crimes during this period. Young women should seek advice from parents or other responsible adults who can help them through these difficult moments.

Menopause

Menopause is a topic that I had to go out of my way to understand for obvious reasons. What I'm about to share with you has come straight from women close to me who were willing to share some of their experiences. The term *menopause* defines a period in a woman's life when her menstruation cycle ceases; it normally occurs some time between the ages of 45–55. This time will vary depending on the health and the biological and genetic makeup of the female. Women generally cannot conceive a child during this period. This is a very difficult time for many women because there are numerous physical transitions that go on inside the body. Hot flashes, mood swings, and loss of sex drive can all be major adjustments during this time. As I said before, this is not my area and I'm not a medical doctor so if you need more help in this area, consult your physician.

Physical Fitness

Not very many people I know can say that they enjoy exercising, including me. I don't like it. Frankly speaking, I do very little of it. I'm not sure at what age exercise helps the most, but I do know it is a good thing to do. Maybe when I start feeling my joints ache I will get a professional trainer to motivate me. If you exercise right, it will cause you to ache, but I suppose that is what it's designed to do. During my military experience, exercise was a way of life. Every morning began with rigorous exercises and running for miles. I do believe I will get back to that lifestyle one day.

The apostle Paul said, "Bodily exercise profiteth little" (1 Tim. 4:8), but he did not say it doesn't help at all. Unless you have a rigorous type of job that forces you to activate the most vital parts of your body such as the cardiovascular system and muscles, you need to exercise often. My dad is in his eighties and he is still as strong as a teenager. He does manual labor, drives tractors and trucks, drives long distances on the road, and anything else he feels like doing. At fifty I don't have the energy he has. Your body was designed for activity, and working until the sweat comes from your brow will not hurt you.

Eating and Dieting

Eating healthy is a real challenge in a society with a fast food joint on every corner. It really takes a strong constitution to resist the urge of constant fast food. I would suggest that you seek the help of a professional who can help you get started from where you are. Natural health is the wave of the future and you'll be able to find someone in your area to help you with nutrition if you try. Please don't forget that greed seems to be the driving force behind our culture in almost everything, so even before you go health food crazy, talk to God first, and verify your heath food.

Read Up

Reading should really be the favorite pastime for a child of destiny. Read wholesome materials that will build your spirit and body. It's OK to read about current affairs but don't get caught up in soap operas. They will drain you of your energy and teach you the wrong values. In fact, limit your time when it comes to the television and secular magazines. As we talked about in the previous steps, very little that comes on the screen is wholesome. You can go to the library and find good healthy books that will help you become an expert in keeping up your holy temple. Your body is the only true temple of God; church is the place where you go to worship and fellowship.

Natural and Spiritual Healing

There is absolutely no question in my mind that God is a healer and that He will heal your body. I have my own testimony to validate His power to heal. However, I do believe that He is very tired of undisciplined, hard-headed, unruly, and lazy saints who think that they can violate the laws of health, yet run to Him every time their belly aches from eating too many sweets and expect Him to work a miracle. The devil is a liar! It's not going to happen. This may sound cold, but you better wake up. People are praying for healing, but they are eating for sickness. If you don't respect the body God gave you, don't expect Him to spoil you with a healing every day when you could do better for yourself. Eating badly will cause you to leave this earth and go to heaven early.

When it comes to natural healing, scientists have discovered that your body in many ways rejuvenates itself over the years. To not believe this is to not believe that Adam, Noah, Methuselah, and others lived long lives. You may not reach nine hundred years of age, but perhaps you can make one hundred. The Bible promised seventy to eighty as a minimum, not maximum, life span. There are hundreds of people living today that are over one hundred and I want to eventually be one of them. I want to go to heaven, but I am not in a hurry. I want to be on the last bus, on the last seat, sleeping. You can laugh about this; it's OK, because I know you're not in a hurry either. I believe that God wants us to live a long, healthy life in this world. Then, when we have become worn out, and not abused out, He will exchange this old temple for our brand new home. We will then enjoy the city that our forefather of faith, Abraham, was looking for—a city of faith, whose builder and maker is God.

The Importance of Fasting

Fasting is one of the hallmarks of a true saint. Sainthood doesn't mean that you go around with a sign on your back looking pious and puritanical; it means that your devotion is directed towards the Father who sees you in secret and rewards you openly. Isaiah 58 is the chapter to check out when you go on a fast. It distinguishes between all those who truly want to fast for the kingdom's sake, and those who want to fast for pride's sake.

Fasting has been a part of my lifestyle for as long as I've been saved. I remember many days seeing my dad go without eating for a greater portion of the day, but I did not really understand why. When I started to embrace the teachings that I was taught as a child, fasting was one of them. Personally, I fast at least one hundred days out of the year. Fasting has both spiritual and natural benefits. There are many people who fast to lose weight or to achieve other health benefits. Fasting is good for you. It is an excellent way to detoxify your body, eliminating excess poison and parasites from your system.

The Bible records two types of fasts—absolute and partial. An absolute fast means to not eat or drink whatsoever for a period of time. A Daniel fast, recorded in Daniel 1, is practiced by many believers as a partial fast.

- It is the exclusion of certain types of food products, especially meat, for a period of time. I believe that a saint should periodically fast if she expects to maintain her spiritual health. Fasting will help you gain strength to break the strongholds of sickness, demons, pride, poverty, or disease in your life. This is the purpose of a God-chosen fast.

Here is what the prophet Isaiah said concerning God's purpose for fasting: "Is it such a fast that I have chosen? a day for a man to afflict his soul? is it to bow down his head as a bulrush, and to spread sackcloth and ashes under him? wilt thou call this a fast, and an acceptable day to the Lord? Is not this the fast that I have chosen? to loose the bands of wickedness, to undo the heavy burdens, and to let the oppressed go free, and that ye break every yoke?" (Isaiah 58:5–6). Fasting will not hurt you, but you must train your body in order to adapt to this type of lifestyle. Begin by fasting for short periods of four to eight hours. Fasting is never going to be comfortable; this is the whole purpose of it. Some people think that missing a meal would be detrimental to them so they consume food nonstop, never giving their body time to detoxify. Fasting is an excellent means of discipline, something that many Christians do not have. Jesus promised His disciples that they would have more power spiritually if they were willing to seek Him through prayer and fasting.

The Superior Woman's Challenge for Chapter 10

1. You only live once, and you will probably only be healthy once. Guard your health because no one else will.

2. Take advantage of the blessing that God has given us in doctors but do not expect them to take the place of God. He is the only one that can give you health, so practice the biblical principles of health in Genesis 1:29.

3. If you are currently battling health issues, with enough discipline and prayer, you can recover your health if you change your lifestyle and develop good health practices.

4. Obesity has more to do with bad eating habits than anything else. Dieting is usually not a lasting cure; if you want to maintain a normal weight level, you must begin to eliminate some things from your diet.

5. A history of health issues such as cancer, high blood pressure, diabetes, or many others in your family is not necessary genetically transferred. Many times it is the result of the same eating habits that are passed down. If your parents or grandparents died from cancer or some other debilitating disease at an early age, you can live a normal life span if you change your traditional diet.

6. If you are single and are suffering from an STD, and you plan to get married, be honest with your mate before committing to marriage.

7. Try to eat home-cooked meals as often as you can, and be sure to monitor your intake of cholesterol, sugar, fats, and other foods that can be unhealthy if too much is consumed.

8. If you cannot join a fitness club, exercise at home and walk often.

Journal

Use this section to log special events (i.e., spiritual breakthroughs, special messages, meeting of new friends, etc.).

Week 1

Week 2

Week 3

Week 4

Study to shew thyself approved unto God, a workman that needeth not be ashamed, rightly dividing the word of truth.

—2 Timothy 2:15

Chapter II

WOMEN IN THE WORD

As women of Zion, you are too valuable to the kingdom to not be skilled in the Word; study to show yourself approved by God and prepared for the world you are called to reach.

THIS PARTICULAR CHAPTER WAS edited into four of the nine books in the Destiny 2000 and Beyond Family Series for two reasons. First, because the material in this chapter is so vital, every saint should be familiar with it, and I did not want to assume that you would read the other books. Secondly, because it is the result of such a tremendous amount of research that it would probably take years of repetitive studying to for you to do this on your own. The information that you will learn in this segment is not generally covered even in a doctorate program. So then, with this in mind, try to glean all you can the first time around and in doing so, it will put you ahead of 90 percent of those who consider themselves students of the Word. This information did not come clear to me until after I had been ministry for ten or more years.

To not understand this aspect of the Bible would be tantamount to not understanding your multiplication table—your future would be crippled without it. Every great building is required to have a viable fire escape route in the event of a fire. If a fire breaks out, the escape route is designed to get you out of the building safely. If you didn't know the fire escape route, your next option would be to jump out of the window. If the only thing you can do with your Bible is quote Scripture, it is like jumping out of the window during a fire. Knowing the chronological sequence of the Bible is like taking the escape route. If you had to jump out of the window, this would be better than dying, but why jump when you can navigate your way out through a charted course?

The Biblical Storyline

The Bible can better serve us if we understand its underlying message. It is a book of redemption. The entire book tells the story of the process which God used to bring fallen humanity back into a right relationship with Himself. When the first man Adam sinned against God, he fell from grace, and God immediately resorted to a backup plan to bring mankind back to Himself. Genesis 3:15 says, "And I will put enmity between thee and the woman, and between thy seed and her seed; it shall bruise thy head, and thou shalt bruise his heel." God started the process by attempting to cleanse the earth of the corrupted seed. When Adam sinned, it polluted the bloodstream of mankind. Man's very nature was corrupted with sin and there was only one remedy: he needed a transformation.

When you read the genealogy of the Bible, you will see that God wanted to keep the bloodline in which the righteous seed would continue. Notice that the righteous seed would come from Adam through Abel and not through Cain. Cain was cursed by God, making his bloodline incapable of furthering the process of redemption.

Notice that God did not curse Adam for his sin, but he was punished with manual labor. Cain however was cursed and this is why the redemption process began with Abel through Adam and not Cain through Adam. Genesis 4:9–11 says, "And the LORD said unto Cain, where is Abel thy brother? And he said, I know not: Am I my brother's keeper? And he said, What hast thou done? the voice of thy brother's blood crieth unto me from the ground. And now art thou cursed from the earth, which hath opened her mouth to receive thy brother's blood from thy hand." Every aspect of the remaining books, chapters, and verses is an attempt to portray and explain God's plan for redeeming man. With the exception of some prophecies that are unclear to us, there is no real mystery about understanding the Bible. You need only know that it is a book of faith, and without faith in God you will never understand it.

Always remember that our standard Bible is not assembled in chronological order. It was printed in logical order to associate similar writings. All of the books of law, history, poetry, and the major and minor prophets are grouped together. The writings of the prophets are not in sequence. If you study and associate the dates and times in which they spoke, you will see that they are not in order.

If you intend to become an avid student of the Bible it is absolutely imperative for you to master the storyline. Again, it is comparable to learning your multiplication table in mathematics. Aside from having a chronological Bible, you need to invest in a Bible that has the historical background and the dates of each book. Always remember to associate the information of each book that you are reading with the subtopic in the storyline. Each book is placed under the subtopic in order to help you remember how to apply the writings in it. When you study the Book of Chronicles you will find that it contains information from the creation of Adam to the restoration period of the Jews, and most of the writings are a repetition of 1 and 2 Samuel and 1 and 2 Kings. No dates are to be considered totally accurate to the very year.

How to Study Your Bible

Always remember to ask these five questions during your study:

1. Who wrote the text?

2. To whom was it written?

3. When was it written?

4. For what purpose was it written?

5. How does it apply to my life?

The Simple Storyline

God created man; man fell from grace; humanity became corrupted; God destroyed the earth with a flood; Abraham was called to establish a nation; his descendents were in bondage for four hundred years in Egypt; Moses was called to deliver them out of Egypt; they wandered in the wilderness for forty years before possessing the Promised Land under the leadership of Joshua; they were led by judges for four hundred years; Samuel was the last judge who anointed the first king whose name was Saul; David succeeded Saul and David's son Solomon succeeded him; after the death of Solomon the nation was divided in two, with Jeroboam, Solomon's servant, leading the ten northern tribes of Israel, and Rehoboam, Solomon's son, leading the two southern tribes, which became known as Judah. Weakened by corrupt leaders, the northern kingdom was captured by the Assyrians in 721 BC. In 586 BC the Babylonians destroyed the temple and carried the choice men of Judah into slavery. After seventy years without a temple, Ezra and Nehemiah led the first expedition to restore the temple. In 516 BC, the Jews resumed public worship in their restored temple.

Creation and Fall
God created the first man, Adam, and placed him in the Garden of Eden. As a result of disobedience and sin God punished Adam and banned him from the garden. Genesis 1–6; date: 4000–2000 BC.

The flood
Because of man's continuous sin God regretted that he had created man. He called Noah to build an ark to save the lives of him and his family during the great flood which covered the earth. Genesis 6–11; date: 2000 BC.

Promise of a nation and bondage in Egypt
God called Abram, changed his name to Abraham, and promised to make him a great nation. This promise was sealed by a covenant of cir-

cumcision. Before the promise would come to fruition, his descendants would be in bondage in Egypt for four hundred years. Genesis 12–50 and the Book of Job; date: 1867–1462 BC.

Deliverance from Egypt and forty years in the wilderness
Moses was born during the period of bondage and spent the first forty years of his life in the house of Pharaoh. In defense of his Hebrew brother he accidentally killed a man and was forced to flee for his life. After spending almost forty additional years in Midian, God called him during a burning bush experience. After he made a covenant commitment with God he accepted the call to go and lead his people out of Egypt. Exodus, Leviticus, Numbers, and Deuteronomy; date: 1462–1442 BC.

Possession of the Promised Land
Moses led the children of Israel into the wilderness where they spent the next forty years. The journey should have only taken two weeks, but because of sin and rebellion it took forty years. Joshua, Moses' successor, was responsible for leading the nation into the Promised Land. Joshua 1–24 and the beginning of Psalms; date: 1422 BC.

The period of the judges
During the period of the judges the children of Israel were led by thirteen judges of whom the last was Samuel. The judges were military leaders who were raised up by God to lead the nation in battle against their enemies. This period lasted about four hundred years before the nation requested a king to lead them. Ruth 1–4, Judges 1–21; date: 1422–1065 BC.

The life of Samuel
Samuel was the last of the judges and the first writing prophet to the Hebrew nation. Samuel's birth reveals the great faith of his mother Hannah. She was barren for many years, but she prayed and pleaded for a child to take away her reproach. Samuel was an answer to prayer, and she vowed to give him to God if he blessed her with a son. As Samuel grew older, his sons were not fit to lead. The elders of Israel requested a

king. God told him to anoint Saul as the first king of Israel. First Samuel 1–28, Psalms, and Chronicles; date: 1100–1060 BC.

The life of King Saul
Saul was anointed by the prophet Samuel to become the first king of Israel. Saul's father was Kish, from the tribe of Benjamin. He started out as a good king but his pride caused him to lose the throne. When he refused to obey the words of the Lord, God rejected him and told Samuel to anoint David to become the next king of Israel. First Samuel 9–31, Psalms, and Chronicles; date: 1065–1025 BC.

The life of King David
David was anointed to become king at a very early age, but he did not sit on the throne until the death of Saul. He served Saul even though he knew that the kingdom was promised to him. David's father, Jesse, was from the tribe of Judah. He was a good king, but he fell into sin when he lusted after Bathsheba, the wife of Uriah. He committed adultery with her and fathered a son whom the Lord declared would not live. David commanded his general, Joab, to put Uriah in the heat of battle to have him killed. God sent the prophet Nathan to tell David that what he had done was in secret but that he was going to expose him. David realized that God knew his dirty little secret, which had turned into a national scandal and disaster. He couldn't hide anything from God. Because David was basically a good man he knew what he needed to do at this point in his political career, which was to come clean. David immediately repented of his sin and fell in the hands of God for judgment. After the death of Uriah, David took Bathsheba to be his wife and Solomon was born from this union. At David's request, Solomon took the throne at his death. First Samuel 16–31, 2 Samuel 1–24, 1 Kings 1, Psalms, and 1 and 2 Chronicles; date: 1025–985 BC.

The life of King Solomon
Solomon became the third king of Israel after the death of his father David. David united Israel but Solomon expanded the kingdom to a

greater degree than his father. He built the first temple in Israel and his fame reached as far as Ethiopia. Solomon became known as the wisest man in the world. As his kingdom increased so did his love for foreign women. When Solomon got old his foreign wives turned his heart against the Lord. For this he paid a great price. God told him that his kingdom would be split in two. At his death the ten northern tribes split off under the leadership of his servant Jeroboam and became known as Israel. The two southern tribes followed his son Rehoboam and became known as Judah. First Kings 1–11, Song of Solomon, Ecclesiastes, Proverbs, Psalms, 1 and 2 Chronicles; date: 945–980 BC.

The divided kingdom to the fall and captivity of Israel
Under Solomon's leadership Israel became a world power. The favor of God was upon this nation because of the commitment that He made to their forefather Abraham. But after Solomon's death, Israel had a succession of weak leaders. This period was the beginning of the nation's downfall. God raised up prophets to warn the nation of its impending doom, but the warning was not heeded. Ahaz was king of Judah who reigned about the year 717 BC before the Assyrians captured the northern kingdom of Israel. During this period the following prophets prophesied: Obadiah, Joel, Jonah, Hosea, Amos, and Micah. Also read 1 and 2 Kings and 1 and 2 Chronicles; date: 945–721 BC.

The fall and captivity of Judah
The southern kingdom of Judah lasted approximately one hundred twenty-five years before it succumbed to the Babylonians. Zedekiah was the last king to reign in Judah before it fell. Under the leadership of Nebuchadnezzar, the Babylonians destroyed the temple in Jerusalem and the Jews were without a temple for seventy years; the temple fell in 587 BC and worship was not restored until 516 BC. Micah, Isaiah, Jeremiah, Lamentations, Zephaniah, Nahum, Habakkuk, Daniel, Ezekiel, 1 and 2 Chronicles, and 2 Kings; date: 600–521 BC.

The restoration period
During the restoration period, the Jews began to return to their homeland. Ezra and Nehemiah were mainly responsible for leading the Jews to restore temple worship. Haggai, Zechariah, and Nehemiah encouraged the nation to build and restore the worship of Jehovah among the people. Esther was also recorded during the restoration period, but this book records the history of the Jews in the city of Susa. Susa, or Sushan, was a province in Persia where the Jews lived under Persian rule.

Malachi is the last book in the Old Testament and it records the worship of the Jews after they were settled back in Jerusalem. He rebuked the nation for not holding to the true worship that God required. He also reminded them of their financial responsibility to the house of God. Haggai, Ezra, Nehemiah, Esther, and Malachi; date: 521–400 BC

After Malachi, the last of the Old Testament prophets, came four hundred silent years. I call the years silent because they left no biblical record; however, this does not suggest that there was no activity in the Jewish nation. This is far from the truth. During the silent years of Jewish history God was still at work in the lives of His people. Persia was still a world power under Artaxerses I, but the nation had begun to weaken. After four thousand years of dominance from the east, the seat of power was shifting to the west. Alexander the Great overthrew Persia and Greece became a world power from 333 to 63 BC. He treated the Jews well and gave them much leisure within the empire.

History of the Jews during the inter-testament period
The term *Jew* was given to the children of Israel, probably as a slang term before it became popular. After the Babylonian captivity, this term replaced the term *Israelite*. This probably happened because Judah remained strong for over a century after the northern kingdom of Israel fell to the Assyrians. As the small band of remnants sought to recover after many years of near extinction, God was still working in their favor.

The Babylonians eventually succumbed to the control of the Persians and the Persians to the Greeks. Greek culture had become a threat to the Jewish spiritual identity. Greece was not so much a military threat as a cultural threat. Greek tradition had become dominant within the Persian Empire and the Jews found themselves being drawn into idolatry once again. The Greeks did not have a central figure to whom they gave religious worship, but it was a culture of superstition and pantheism. Many Jews settled in Alexandria, Egypt, which was under Greek domination. Hellenism was a major stronghold in this city.

One of the philosophical views of Greek culture was called stoicism. Epicureanism, another philosophy, encouraged its followers to avoid sexual excess if they wanted to truly enjoy life. It encouraged friendship and love for one's fellow man.

As the Jews sought to regain a strong sense of their religious heritage, a group called the Scribes had begun to place great emphasis on the teaching of Jewish laws. By the second century BC, another group known as the Pharisees, or "ones who separated themselves," began to reassert the observance of worship in smaller settings. The synagogues were the main places of assembly. They taught that the belief in angels, demons, and the resurrection of the dead should be observed by all those who truly believed in God.

Another group with a view opposed to the Pharisees became known as the Sadducees. This was a smaller group of the priestly lineage who primarily controlled worship in the temple. The Sadducees would not embrace any teaching which could not be validated from the law or canon. The canon was known as "an authoritative list for a given community." This group opposed the resurrection, as well as belief in angels and demons.

A Syrian ruler by the name of Antiochus IV Epiphanies was determined to force Greek culture upon the Jews. In his conflict with the Jews, it is said that he went into the temple and sacrificed a pig on the altar. This was considered sacrilege because Jews did not eat pork—it was considered unclean.

In the Apocrypha, the story is told of a Jewish family called the Maccabees who lived about the year 150 BC who fought for Jewish independence. Judas Maccabeus was the prominent leader in the family.

Most of these activities took place in and around the city of Jerusalem. The book of Maccabees records many of the psalms of their victories against their enemies as well as prayers and lamentations.

The Romans conquered the Greeks and became a world power about the year 64 BC, but Greek culture remained dominant in Judea for many years after Roman domination. Even in the midst of the Jewish struggles, there was a small remnant that remained faithful to the God of their forefathers. They longed for the day when the Messiah would come as predicted by the prophets and throw off the yokes of their foreign oppressors.

It was foretold more than seven hundred years before the birth of Jesus that the Messiah would be born in the city of Bethlehem. The prophets foretold of His birth and crucifixion. According to the prophet Isaiah, He would be called the suffering servant. He would come in great humility and suffering in order to make the final atonement for the sins of the nation. For about three and a half years, Jesus pursued His ministry, teaching the restoration of the kingdom of Israel. He taught, preached, and healed many people of their sickness and disease. He was the son of Mary and Joseph. Joseph, according to the New Testament, was a carpenter by trade. Several doubts were voiced about the authenticity of Jesus and his ministry because he did not come from the ruling priestly lineage of the Jewish hierarchy.

Great skepticism arose about His claim to be the "King of the Jews." He gained the respect of the common people while being derided by and suffering great disdain from both the Pharisees and the Sadducees. Early in my ministry I was told a little story about the two parties and how to always distinguish the difference between the two. The Sadducees were sad, you see, because they did not believe in the resurrection. The Pharisees were fair you see, because they believed in the resurrection. Jesus foretold His own death, burial, and resurrection, and just as He predicted, the Bible records His death, resurrection, and ultimate ascension back to the Father in Acts 1. His disciples took seriously the charge of carrying His message to the four corners of the earth.

The New Testament
The New Testament begins with the Gospels of Matthew, Mark, Luke and John. The first three are known as the synoptic Gospels, meaning their narratives are similar. The four writers give us a look at the birth, public ministry, rejection, crucifixion and resurrection of Jesus. Matthew, Mark, Luke, and John. 40–60 CE.

Acts is considered the historical book of the New Testament. With the exception of the four Gospels and the Book of Revelation, all of the other books in the New Testament were written within the same period as Acts. Romans, 1 and 2 Corinthians, Galatians, Ephesians, Philippians, Colossians, 1 and 2 Thessalonians, 1 and 2 Timothy, Titus, Philemon, Hebrews, James, and 1 and 2 Peter 1–2.

The Book of Revelation
The Book of Revelation is perhaps the most controversial book in the Bible because so much of its content has to do with things to come. It is inclusive of some of the writings of Daniel and Ezekiel. The early disciples, including the disciples of Jesus, were expecting Him to return in their lifetimes. It is evident in the history of the New Testament church that the lifestyles of its members had begun to take the shape of those who were expecting the Messiah to return soon. They sold their possessions and developed a community of believers. When it seemed as if Jesus' return was being delayed many of the disciples started to lose faith. Peter cautioned against this doubting spirit:

> Knowing this first, that there shall come in the last days scoffers, walking after their own lusts, And saying, Where is the promise of his coming? for since the fathers fell asleep, all things continue as they were from the beginning of the creation. For this they willingly are ignorant of, that by the word of God the heavens were of old, and the earth standing out of the water and in the water: Whereby the world that then was, being overflowed with water, perished: But the heavens and the earth, which are now, by the same word are kept in store, reserved unto fire against the day of judgment

and perdition of ungodly men. But, beloved, be not ignorant of this one thing, that one day is with the Lord as a thousand years, and a thousand years as one day. The Lord is not slack concerning his promise, as some men count slackness; but is longsuffering to us-ward, not willing that any should perish, but that all should come to repentance. But the day of the Lord will come as a thief in the night.

—2 Peter 3:3–10

Prior to Y2K, I sat and listened to the prognosis of those who were trying to convince me that they knew all about the time when the Lord would return, or about what tribulation period was at hand. It was quite amusing. I thought, *How can anybody read the Bible and get so far off base?* If you polled a thousand people and asked them to give their take on the subject, depending on the extent of their answers, you may get one thousand different views.

When Y2K was swiftly approaching, I was still in possession of my radio station. Preachers from all over the country were predicting everything from the rapture, Armageddon, food shortages, and the blacking out of the major cities in the world. They sold thousands of books, tapes, and videos, frightening people into depression. We were told to dig a well in the backyard and fill our cellar with food. I thought to myself how unfair this would be, because four billion of the six billion people in the world don't know what they're going to eat the next day, and how long can you last on a few canned goods anyway? The preachers took the profit from the books and tapes and when nothing happened at the turn of the millennium, nobody repented of their misdirection and the profit received from the sale of books and tapes was not refunded.

Time alone will reveal what God's ultimate plan is for mankind. Some things are very clear in Scripture but others are quite vague. It is futile to spend too much time debating how we will live in the future when we haven't yet learned how to live in the present. I believe that the best thing for us to do as believers is to live the best lives we can from day to day. Your judgment day starts at your death. If it takes Jesus another millennium to return, He will not have done any injustice. His words are clear in terms of what He expects out of us while He tarries. If He wanted us to know a specific day, I believe He would have left a specific date on the record.

Jesus gently rebukes His disciples in Acts 1:6–9 for wanting to know the exact day of his ultimate triumph: "When they therefore were come together, they asked of him, saying, Lord, wilt thou at this time restore again the kingdom to Israel? And he said unto them, It is not for you to know the times or the seasons, which the Father hath put in his own power. But ye shall receive power, after that the Holy Ghost is come upon you: and ye shall be witnesses unto me both in Jerusalem, and in all Judaea, and in Samaria, and unto the uttermost part of the earth. And when he had spoken these things, while they beheld, he was taken up; and a cloud received him out of their sight."

May your journey through the Bible be one of joy and delight. God gave us His Word to help make our walk of faith more pleasurable. The Book of Revelation is said to have been written between AD 90–110.

The Superior Woman's Challenge for Chapter 11

1. Every believer should have a daily scheduled time of prayer and devotion. Your devotion should include reading and singing. Set aside twenty to thirty minutes daily to be alone with God.

2. Most Christians do not understand the Bible because they do not take the time to learn it. You cannot be effective in any area in life unless you are willing to commit to studying and training. You cannot effectively sell a product if you are not familiar with what it entails. Find the time to make this happen so you can be effective in the kingdom of God.

3. You should commit to memory certain books, passages, and individual scriptures in order to combat the enemy when the forces of disbelief, evil, and fear come upon your life.

4. It is imperative that you understand the difference between church denominations and the kingdom of God. In the traditional church, anyone can join at will, but in the kingdom of God, you must be transformed by the power of God before you can enter. John 3 is a good illustration of this principle.

5. Begin to think of ways in which you and your church organization can build your ministry on kingdom principles. This can only happen when you have a working relationship with people from various denominations who are living out kingdom principles.

6. When studying the Old and New Testaments, you must understand that they are not two different books, but one book covering a transition in the history of the Jews. Jesus' entire ministry was directed to the scattered Jews who were having the King restored to them. The teachings of Paul and the other writings in the New Testament tell how this mission was continued by the apostles.

Journal

Use this section to log special events (i.e., spiritual breakthroughs, special messages, meeting of new friends, etc.).

Week 1

Week 2

Week 3

Week 4

I will pour out of my spirit upon all flesh; and your sons and your daughters shall prophesy.

—Joel 2:28

Chapter 12

WOMEN IN MINISTRY

In all my years of ministry, I have never seen a man doing anything that a woman could not do, and sometimes she even does it better.

THE TERM *MINISTRY* BY definition means "to serve," and service is what we have been called to give. Women outnumber men by a three-to-one margin in most service-related areas of ministry. In biblical times, the ministry was dominated by men, but in our era women have held the forefront. When you look at the traditional roles that women fill in the ministry such as pastors, prophetesses, ushers, and greeters—as well as the areas in which they traditionally serve, such as choir, children's church, nursery, evangelism, and youth outreach—not to mention the makeup of the congregation itself, women are in the majority in most of these areas. Joel's prediction that women would prophesy has been fulfilled. When you read in the Book of Acts about the birth of the church, the apostle Peter made it plain when he quoted from the prophet Joel that God was going to use women as well as men in the ministry (Joel 2:28). Women were a part of the group that was in the upper room and were filled with the Holy Spirit and spoke in tongues (Acts 1:14, 15; 2:1, 4). Peter quoted Joel's prediction that this provision was for all whom God calls (Acts 2:23, 38, 39).

The apostle Paul spoke very highly of women being active in ministry, and he personally endorsed their services. Some of the women he endorsed were Phoebe, Pricilla, Andronicus, and Junia. Many other women were also active in the church. Serving is something women enjoy, because it is through serving that they get the joy of giving to God. In addition to the incredible amount of services that women give, they also give their finances freely. As men, we owe you a debt of gratitude for standing in while we were out. In my book titled *God's Man: Son, Servant, Prophet and King*, I challenge men to rise up and become the men God has called them to be. I said to them that our women are tired of seeing us sit back as passive and unconcerned men and want us to become activists in our communities and in our churches.

From the earliest times, women have played a major role in carrying out the ministry. When the children of Israel came out of Egypt, Miriam prophesied to them about the miracle of their deliverance: "And Miriam the prophetess, the sister of Aaron, took a timbrel in her hand; and all the women went out after her with timbrels and with dances. And Miriam answered them, Sing ye to the LORD, for he hath triumphed gloriously; the horse and his rider hath he thrown into the sea" (Exodus 15:20–21).

Throughout Scripture you will find women who were on the cutting edge of what God was doing is the midst of His people. These are the apostle Paul's closing remarks to the church in Galatia. Galatians 3:2–28 says, "For as many of you as have been baptized into Christ have put on Christ. There is neither Jew nor Greek, there is neither bond nor free, there is neither male nor female: for ye are all one in Christ Jesus." Being one in Christ means having His Spirit and vision. He has liberated women to participate in the ministry.

Sunday School Teachers, Children's Ministry

For each of the ministry roles mentioned above, as well as in other portions of this book, my hope and prayer is that this series for women will be the catalyst for mentoring strong women to serve in these intricate areas of ministry. Each of the individual ministries must be filled with qualified women who have been trained to work in it. The time has passed for merely allowing people to walk in and choose their area of service. God is requiring the leaders of ministries to be responsible for the types of people that are allowed to serve over His flock. If you have been asked to serve, or are serving in one of the areas above, be sure that you ask for proper training before being put to work. Serving in ministry can become very frustrating if you have not been specifically told what is expected of you.

As part of the Destiny 2000 and Beyond Family Series, we have designed a book that will help you with structure when you are working with children. I recommend that you get a copy if you are working with children. I cannot say enough about the tremendous amount of help that women provide in these areas; without you, there would probably not even be a children's ministry. I want to personally thank you for what you do as well as encourage you to keep up the good work. God will reward you for your labor. Sometimes the ministry can be demanding on your life, but God sees the sacrifices that you make from week to week, and He will not let you go unrewarded.

The entire Destiny 2000 and Beyond Family Series was birthed out of a need to take the strain out of ministry. For years I struggled to find appropriate and current topics that I could use to implement teaching and training for our ministry, and this series is by far the best tool that I have discovered. I want you to continue seeking God for innovative things that you can do to keep the ministry that you do interesting and captivating for the children and youth that you serve. Our children are no longer the church of tomorrow but the church of today.

Teaching should be fun, and your level of confidence in what you do helps make what you do fulfilling and rewarding. No amount of money can compensate you for being fulfilled when you are working in the kingdom of God. If there are no finances allocated in the ministry for what you do, nevertheless put your heart into what you do, and God will meet your material and financial need from somewhere else. Continue to serve your organization with a heart full of love for God and the leadership team to whom you have been assigned. I have seen people who served out of wrong motives, and they became frustrated and threw in the towel. Be sure that your personal life is in order before you commit to serve, because if it's not, your ministry activity will further frustrate you and cause the devil to wreak havoc in your life as well in the ministry in which you desire to serve. May the blessings and peace of God be upon your life as you serve.

Ushering

It has been said that ushering and greeting are two of the most important areas of ministry. If the people coming through the doors of the church are not treated with the utmost care and respect, they will probably never return. Ushering should be taken just as seriously as preaching. As an usher, you can make just the right impact on a visitor that may draw them to the ministry where you are serving. I have seen some ushers who were outright rude. They act as if they are policemen at the front of the church. If the people who are coming act rudely or out of character, the ushers would sink to their level. I reminded the ushers in our ministry that it was not their job to get on the same level as people who act out of character and don't know how to behave in a public setting.

If you are trying to instruct a person to sit in a particular area and they refuse to do so, do not get into a shouting match with the individual. Allow them to sit where they choose unless it is hazardous for them to do so. If it will cause a grave problem, get someone from the security team or one of the deacons or stewards and allow them to do their job. This will salvage your relationship with the disgruntled person and allow you as an usher to maintain a level of professionalism. As an usher, you are not part of the security team, so don't allow yourself to be drawn into this type of altercation.

Women especially should be cordial and sweet even if they have to do it in a tactful way. This side of women should be accented while on duty. If holding your post as an usher is so stressful that you become unable to be kind, you need to ask to be excused from the floor until you can settle what it is that is troubling you. As an usher, you are in place to welcome the parishioners and visitors into the house of God, not your house. You must know how to treat your guests when they arrive. This is why training is necessary for every area of ministry.

You should not be offended when you are asked to take classes before you are put in position to serve in the church. It is interesting to see how people who would not have a second thought about being trained to work a secular job become offended when you ask them to submit themselves for training in the house of the Lord. Churches that are desperate to put people in position and refuse to make them accountable first are compromising the ethics of biblical stewardship. David declared that being a doorkeeper in the house of the Lord was a very rewarding place to serve. Ushering in the house of the Lord will get you the same reward that some high-ranking church official will receive because heaven is a level playing field. We will all be servants when we get there.

Music, Choirs, and Praise and Worship Singers

The music ministry is arguably the most powerful ministry in the church. I say arguably because in some people's eyes, it is above the ministry of the Word. Of course, I don't agree. I would say it comes second to praying and preaching. Every major religious organization embraces the ministry of music in one form or another. In this aspect of the ministry, women once again are the dominant force. Perhaps more musicians are male, but when it comes to the choir, the praise and worship singers, praise dancers, and the other music-oriented functions, women lead the way. In antiquity, this area was exclusively controlled by men. In biblical times the Levites were responsible for the worship and praise segment of temple worship. This was a responsibility given to the Levites by God when He gave Moses the organizational structure for the nation. They were not allowed to own any part of the land that was given to the other eleven tribes. The Levites were the priests, musicians, singers, and custodians of the temple. During this time, women were relegated to the home for the most part and served as helpers in maintaining the community.

Since the turn of the twentieth century, during the rebirth of Pentecostalism in the United States and across the world, women have made a tremendous impact in every facet of the ministry. The music ministry, like all other areas where women are very strong, has been influenced by their desire to serve. This area is probably the most controversial area in the church. It is volatile and fickle because it is a breeding ground for all types of spirits. I think that more people collectively are attracted to this area than any other area in the church. Due to the fact that music from its inception on Earth was orchestrated by Lucifer, one of the archangels that fell from grace, it attracts all types of spirits. When he fell from grace and was expelled from heaven, the Bible said his influence was so vast that a third of the heavenly angels were spoiled by him. In my many years in church and ministry, I have seen all kinds of people who aspire to work in the music ministry.

People seem to think that all they have to do is come to church, give the preacher their hand, and join the choir. Frankly, we have permitted this to happen even to this day. Several years ago I took inventory of what was happening in my ministry in the area of music, and I totally revolutionized the way I approached this ministry. No longer will I allow anyone to sing on the choir or join my music staff unless they have been totally processed into the ministry, which takes months. People should be thoroughly proven before entering this area of the church. It is no place for people who are not spiritually stable. An unstable music ministry will breed an unstable ministry overall. If the musicians and singers are allowed to live loose lives, the ministry will be no better.

Evangelists

Women serving in the roles of evangelists and missionaries have probably one of the most frustrating jobs in the church. It is frustrating because the church, the body of Christ, has yet to capture the importance of this role. Many of the churches that have been birthed over the years owe their existence to women. Unfortunately, once many of the women are finished birthing the church, they are long forgotten by pastors who come along to reap the benefits. If the church, the body of Christ, would embrace the anointing that is upon these women who are willing to go to great lengths to reach a soul, it would continue to fund them and keep them doing what they have been called to do. The trap that the enemy has used is forcing true evangelists and missionaries to become pastors; as a result, the ministry is stunted. I continue to use the term *body of Christ* because we are short-sighted by our organizations. I wholeheartedly endorse and believe in church denomination. It helps with structure as a result of many years of experience in the ministry. However, when any ministry or organization deviates from the Bible, or sets itself up to be the only right way, God will judge it. One of the other big issues facing us today is the problem of true believers being limited for the sake of the other members' ability to work in harmony. This is a barrier that religious organizations and denominations have put up over the past four to five hundred years. Prior to this, the Roman Catholic church dominated the church world for nearly one thousand years and made it a political fighting machine, something that Jesus warned His disciples against.

Now that we have come through two major eras in the church world, where do we go from here? Almost every intelligent spiritual believer knows that God did not call His church to division. Many of us know that the time has come for the true church to tear down its walls just as the communist Berlin Wall and various racial barriers had to come down in our modern era. We are at a crossroads in the church and God is calling for His kingdom to come. When the kingdom comes, it will not be known by color, organization, or national boundaries; it will be known by the love and working relationship it has across the barriers that divide us. When this happens, the evangelists, missionaries, pastors, bishops, apostles, and whatever other titles people stand behind, will be functioning like armed forces. In wartime, the army, air force, navy, and marines all work together for a single cause. We can put the evangelists and missionaries to work on the street corners of every community in our nation for the benefit of winning souls for the kingdom of God—not for the benefit of a group of self-serving leaders who cannot see beyond their local church borders. It is time for the kingdom to come on Earth as it is in heaven and God is going to do it with or without those who will not heed His calling.

Pastors

For women, the pastorate, like all other male-dominated fields, has been and still is a tough hill to climb. First of all, you have to sort through your own prohibitions that have been passed on as a result of tradition. For years I have listened to women who testified how long it took them to follow God's leading because they were worried about what people would think of them going into the pastorate. Throughout this book I've said that I believe a woman can do anything in the ministry that a man can do. It is my understanding that our ministries belong to God, and if He could use a jackass to speak to Balaam and a rooster to speak to Peter, He can use a woman to preach to a congregation. On the other hand, the mere ability to preach, teach, and minister from the pulpit does not necessarily make a woman a pastor. The same holds true for men.

I think that too many people have approached the pastorate for the wrong reason. It is wrong for you to strive to get into the pastorate just because you are out to prove what you can do. Bad motives are what got the church in the predicament it is in today. The competitiveness, strife, jealousy, and egotism that are at the forefront of many ministries are the reasons why the body of Christ is so fragmented and weak. Church members make up a majority in basically every community in America, yet we are still led around by the nose by lying and deceiving politicians. The Bible says that we should be the head and not the tail, but because we are so fragmented and torn apart by schisms, we are powerless in any given municipality.

If you truly believe that you have been called to pastor or if you are currently pastoring, I want to encourage you to seek God for His direction for your ministry. You really need to understand kingdom principles in place of what you have been taught by the traditional church.

God is ushering in a new paradigm for His church and He is expecting His leaders to follow the shift. The New Testament church had five foundational principles given to them by Christ during His three and a half years of ministry—worship, ministry, discipleship, fellowship, and evangelism. These principles know no racial, denominational or national boundaries. If the church, the body of Christ, is going to be effective in winning this generation, we must break down our barriers and work in ministry together. If you understand the necessity of this task and are willing to dedicate the time needed to stay in touch with God, you can be successful at your calling. Building a large church should not be your goal; building a healthy church is what's important. Bigger does not necessarily mean better for a church any more than being fat means a person is healthy. Jesus died to build a body of believers from every race, nation, and tongue, bound together by love and motivated to serve all humanity. We are not called to be one in name, but we must become one in Spirit. We must collectively impact our communities for God.

First Ladies

First ladies—whether they are pastors' wives, superintendents' wives, bishops' wives, overseers' wives, apostles' wives, priests' wives, or the wife of any leading man in the ministry—play a pivotal role in the success of that ministry. First ladies can actually make or break the ministry. This is not to say that God will not use their husbands, but their success can be greatly enhanced or impaired by their wives. I am a preacher's kid and a pastor, so I know firsthand how important it is for the first lady to work in harmony with her husband. Over the years, I watched my mom following closely with my dad in every aspect of the ministry. As a lad I had no clue what all of this meant, but when I became an adult and was called into the ministry and ultimately the pastorate, it all came full circle. Due to the overwhelming amount of women in the church, a leading lady who can serve as a sort of model is extremely important to have. This also holds true for men. The more I learn about God and His purpose for the church, it is clear to me that His ultimate goal is to restore to mankind what was lost in the Garden of Eden. What must be modeled is the loving relationship between a man and a woman that was lost as a result of sin.

When parishioners come to church, many of them look to the church leadership for the model or the lack thereof that they have at home. Wearing the hat of a first lady is no easy role to say the least, but God will give you grace to do the job if your heart is with your husband. When the husband and wife have a good relationship, this same spirit will trickle down to the membership. This is why it is so important for the first family to be intact. It is hard to teach principles when you aren't an example of them.

As a first lady, you must be on your toes at all times because the enemy is out to destroy your family relationship. The better your relationship is, the harder your fight will be in this area. You must have a good understanding of your responsibilities to God and your husband, and of what you are called to do in the ministry that you are planted. If you are unsure about who you are in any of these areas, you will have a very hard time functioning as a first lady. I recommend that you seek the mentorship of other first ladies who have proven records of success in all three areas and can help you to be successful in your role. One of the things that is key for a first lady is to have the good of the people at heart. No one wants to feel as if they are just being tolerated rather than loved. It sends the wrong message to your followers if it appears as if you are there just because your husband is there. To be a first lady can be very rewarding, provided you understand that you will sometimes suffer just because of who you are. When you understand this, you can take it gracefully and not become bitter or hardened by what the enemy will try to ensnare you with. This is no role for the timid or faint-hearted; you must be a spiritual warrior. But if you can master spiritual warfare, you will make it in this role.

The Superior Woman's Challenge for Chapter 12

1. Contrary to what many people have been made to believe about ministry, it is not limited to the individuals with titles. All of us are called to ministry in one way or another. All were not called to pastor or to be prophets, but serving is a fundamental responsibility of every believer.

2. In light of the above statement, what specific aspect of ministry do you believe you've been called to? How are you pursuing this area of your life?

3. Understanding and implementing kingdom principles in our lives is imperative. If you do not thoroughly understand how this works, you need to ask God to put you in the path of someone who does.

4. Consider some ways to connect and work with other ministries that are not a part of your local church or denomination. This is a kingdom principle that must be fostered among all believers.

5. You do not need a certificate of ordination to join the ranks of women in ministry. The following scriptures are clear statements of Jesus' position on women serving in ministry. After His resurrection an angel appeared first to women and gave them the task of telling the good news to the disciples (Matthew 28:5–11). And Joel 2:28 says, "And it shall come to pass afterward, that I will pour out my spirit upon all flesh; and your sons and your daughters shall prophesy, your old men shall dream dreams, your young men shall see visions."

6. This is your final challenge for this particular book: visit all twelve sections in your journal in order to fine-tune those areas you want to remember.

Journal

Use this Journal section to log special events (i.e., spiritual breakthroughs, special messages, meeting of new friends, etc.)

Week 1

Week 2

Week 3

Week 4

About the Author and the Birthing of Destiny

The Destiny 2000 and Beyond Family Series was birthed through the leading of the Holy Spirit in March of 2005. The writer was awakened at about 3:00 a.m. and the Spirit of God began to dictate the words he was to write. The writer had no idea at the time that a full blown vision was underway. Within twenty days, book number four, *Rite of Passage*, was written. Within ninety days, the writer was inspired to write the three children's books and the marriage journal. By the end of December 2005 the writer was inspired to pen four other books: *God's Man: Prophet, Priest, King*, *How to Live Single, Saved, and Happy*, *God's Superior Woman*, and *Starting Over After a Divorce*.

The writer believes that it is futile to take any credit for the unveiling of this grand vision since it was totally the working of the Holy Spirit of God. Due to the polarization of religious organizations and the great racial divide that exists within the church, emphasis on the writer or the writer's identity would be a distraction in the promulgation of the vision. The principles in the Destiny 2000 and Beyond Family Series transcend religion, race, gender, and nationality. It will actually take the working of the Spirit in your heart for you to understand how the Destiny 2000 and Beyond Family Series will play out in your life, church, or organization. Habakkuk 2:2–3 says, "And the Lord answered me, and said, Write the vision, and make it plain upon tables, that he may run that readeth it. For the vision is yet for an appointed time, but at the end it shall speak, and not lie: though it tarry, wait for it; because it will surely come, it will not tarry." The term *author* by definition means "composer." *Authorize* means to give authority or power to someone. In this light, the writer is only the bearer of the good news; the Holy Spirit is the Author of the Destiny 2000 and Beyond Family Series. May the journey to your destiny be one of prosperity, peace, and pleasure. Writer: Edward Lee Johnson; Author: The Holy Spirit

For more information on how to obtain the Destiny 2000 and Beyond Family Series contact us at:

Web site: www.destiny2000andbeyond.com
E-mail: regionaldirector@destiny2000andbeyond.com
Phone: call the regional director at 843-330-7807

The Destiny 2000 and Beyond Family Series includes the following books, written by Edward Lee Johnson:

Preschool Little Angels
Sunshine Club I
Sunshine Club II
Rite of Passage
How to Live Single, Saved, and Happy
Marriage Journal
God's Man: Prophet, Priest, and King
God's Superior Woman
Starting Over After a Divorce